My Inner Child and the Grief that Made Me: A Memoir Leading to a Revelation of GRACE

By Georgia L. James

Copyright © 2026 Georgia L. James

All rights reserved. No part of this book may be reproduced, distributed, or transmitted in any form or by any means, including photocopying, recording, or other electronic or mechanical methods, without the prior written permission of the publisher, except in the case of brief quotations embodied in critical reviews and certain other noncommercial uses permitted by copyright law.

For permissions requests, write to the publisher at the address below:

MAWMedia Group, LLC
Los Angeles | Reno | Nashville
www.mawmedia.com

Limit of Liability/Disclaimer of Warranty:

While the publisher and author have used their best efforts in preparing this book, they make no representations or warranties with respect to the accuracy or completeness of the contents of this book and specifically disclaim any implied warranties of merchantability or fitness for a particular purpose. The advice and strategies contained herein may not be suitable for your situation. You should consult with a professional where appropriate. Neither the publisher nor author shall be liable for any loss of profit or any other commercial damages, including but not limited to special, incidental, consequential, or other damages.

ISBN: 978-1-943616-81-7

# Dedication

Dr. Michael A. Wright, thank you for your wisdom, dedication, direction, and most importantly for believing in me. You have truly inspired me to do my best and to always remain true to myself, and for that I thank you. To have true happiness is living with authenticity, this is what has helped me through many difficult moments and decisions. And I want to thank you for always helping me keep this a priority in my life. I will never forget my 1st year at TSU, and asking you, "Will I ever know how to speak like you?" I was so amazed and excited all at the same time. I want to thank you for teaching me how to take advantage of the spaces where I find myself and turn them into success. I want to thank you for showing me how to deal with life's struggle in a positive way. I can genuinely say that it is an honor to have a mentor like you. I wish many more great years ahead of you as you continue to bless and teach others with your experience, wisdom, and influence like you did for me.

For my husband Jerall, who always pushes me, who has walked every step of this journey with me. Thank you for never giving up on me, and seeing the potential in me even when i didn't… often. Thank you for being the reason for my happy moments and the comfort to my sad ones. You pay attention to every emotion, and you are the first to wipe my tears. You make everything in my world "perfect." With you by my side, I can conquer the world. With your unwavering support and love, I have nothing to fear. Through every joy, every pain, every struggle, thank you for holding my hand and not letting go. I am blessed to be loved by you.

# Contents

Dedication ............................................................................. 3

Preface: Grief, Resilience, Achievement, Confidence, and Excellence ............................................................................. 6

Prologue: Dear Grandma, ............................................................................. 11

Section I: Leaving for College (Separation) [ 3 Influences ] ............................................................................. 14

Chapter 1: Embracing a New Adventure ............................................................................. 15

Chapter 2: Trouble in a Toxic Paradise ............................................................................. 21

Chapter 3: Seeing Me for the First Time ............................................................................. 28

Chapter 4: New Beginnings and Responsibilities ............................................................................. 35

Section II: Loss of Grandfather, Mother, and Father (Descent) [ 3 Losses ] ............................................................................. 43

Chapter 5: GRACE - Strength amid Struggles ............................................................................. 44

Chapter 6: RESILIENCE - Contemplating the Path Forward ............................................................................. 50

Chapter 7: ACHIEVEMENT - The Legacy From my Parents ............................................................................. 56

Chapter 8: CONFIDENCE - Confirming My Purpose ............................................................................. 62

Chapter 9: EXCELLENCE - New Lessons Rising Above ............................................................................. 66

Section III: Healing My Inner Child ............................................................................. 73

Chapter 10: Self-Discovery with Family Dynamic ............................................................................. 74

Chapter 11: Journey of Healing and Self-Realization ............................................................................. 80

Appendix: Affirmations ............................................................................. 86

Affirmations For Healing Your Inner Child ............................................................................. 87
    Grief ............................................................................. 90
    Resilience ............................................................................. 92
    Achievement ............................................................................. 94
    Confidence ............................................................................. 96
    Excellence ............................................................................. 98
    Faith ............................................................................. 101

Persistence .......................................................................... 104
Leverage .............................................................................. 106
Learning .............................................................................. 109
Courage ............................................................................... 112
Adaptability ........................................................................ 115
Networking ......................................................................... 118

# Preface: Grief, Resilience, Achievement, Confidence, and Excellence

**Contemplating Marriage**

Jerall and I had made the decision to go to the courthouse and get married. As we delved into deep conversations about why I had been dragging my feet and why I didn't want a big, traditional wedding, I started to question my own lack of excitement. While my friends were thrilled for me, I couldn't help but wonder why I wasn't as thrilled as they were. Lately, I also noticed that I was becoming more emotional about my parents, even though they had been gone for years. It was hitting me in a different way, and I needed to process these feelings.

Reflecting on my life and where I am in my career, I can't help but feel like there are missing pieces. I wish my parents were here to witness my achievements and see how everything is coming together for me. My grandmother, who has always been present for every milestone, is now 90 years old and tired. While I am grateful for her support and the fact that she visits my home, which I am still in awe of, I long for my parents' presence. It's bittersweet that they are not here to witness my passion for working in the social work field, although there is still more, I want to accomplish in that realm. What really strikes me is the fact that, after all these years, I am feeling a new kind of pain in their absence.

I shared these thoughts with Jerall, explaining that having a traditional wedding would require me to be given away, and both my mom and dad should be there for that moment. However, the reality is that they are not. I did not want to be walked down the aisle. I had to determine whether I wanted a wedding. A wedding is too much money for an event inviting people who are putting into it. I was more interested in putting that $3000 into a destination wedding with passports, going out of the country, creating an experience.

My family would expect my uncle to give me away, but the truth is, I have never been close to him. As an adult, I struggle with my feelings towards him, and I would choose Jerall to walk me down the aisle if necessary.

My uncle was financially helping my grandmother, but he was emotionally abusive. My grandmother never really stood up for us. He attempts to make up for his behavior today, but he I needed that love and nurture back then. This created some trauma for me. It puts me back in that little girl mode. I work to remember that I am not that little girl anymore. Now that I am trained in mental health, I know that the trauma created fear, hesitation, and self-questioning within me. I challenge that feeling within myself every day.

I needed to get away from that reality. They could not see the vision I had for myself. My uncle is that father figure for all my siblings and cousins. I don't feel that way. I feel a sense of respect now coming from him, but that was not the case growing up.

I know this might result in negative opinions, but it's important for me to stay true to myself and my own truth. I am working on getting out of my feelings about this and focusing on the present moment, where I can own my truth and make decisions that feel right for me. That's one of the primary messages I hope for this book: Those who hurt you must no longer hold you in the place where they hurt you. Even the grief that I felt in the passing of cherished loved ones cannot hold me as I intentionally work through the feelings and endeavor to live authentically.

### Grief, Resilience, Achievement, Confidence, and Excellence

The difference between then and now is the way I perceive things. If my mother were alive today, I wouldn't be angry or resentful towards her. I wouldn't need her for the material aspects of life; instead, I would value and cherish the love and connection we could have. If she needed to move in with me, I would be open to it because the relationship is what matters most. Having my parents here with me would be enough. My success in life was not a generational expectation; I had to pave my own path, educate myself, network, and struggle to affirm my choices. Now, I am fully engaged in life, living it the way I have always wanted. Although there are still aspects I struggle with and areas where I feel like I'm out of my depth, I am here, doing it all, and doing it well.

As a social worker and therapist, I am immersing myself in the world of group home care. I am living in a house, driving my own car, and I have a loving husband and children by my side. I wish my parents could be witnesses to all of this, celebrating my achievements and seeing how far I have come. The resulting reflection is this book.

In the context of the book, here's how each of the constructs - Grief, Resilience, Achievement, Confidence, and Excellence - can be understood based on the outlined chapters:

1. The protagonist reflects on the loss of their grandfather, mother, and father, exploring the deep emotions and challenges of grief. The chapter delves into their pain and

struggle, showcasing their inner strength and journey towards finding support amidst their sorrow.
2. The book emphasizes the recurring theme of resilience, seen in my decision to pursue college despite doubts and reluctance. They also show resilience by persevering in their aspirations despite grief and temptation to give up. My ability to bounce back from adversity is a notable aspect of their journey.
3. Achievement plays a central role in my story, with chapters highlighting their pursuit of education, academic accomplishments, and success in working with group homes. Their determination to achieve their goals and make a positive impact on others' lives is evident throughout the book.
4. Confidence is a crucial element in my growth and development. They gain confidence in the college environment, thanks to the guidance of Dr. Wright, who recognizes their potential and encourages them to reach for their dreams. Overcoming self-doubt and building confidence in their abilities is a significant part of their journey.
5. The book weaves the concept of excellence into my pursuit of personal and professional growth. They strive for excellence in their education and career, overcoming challenges along the way. Chapter 9 focuses on their self-realization, as they work towards personal growth and maintaining excellence in their relationships.

Overall, the book explores the themes of grief, resilience, achievement, confidence, and excellence (GRACE) showcasing my transformative journey and their ability to navigate through adversity to create a fulfilling life despite their losses and challenges.

## Prologue: Dear Grandma,

I want to take a moment to acknowledge the incredible impact you have had on my life. Your strength, resilience, wisdom, and unwavering spirituality have shaped me into the person I am today. In the midst of grief and adversity, you stood strong, guiding and supporting us with your unparalleled love and determination.

The strength you possess is truly remarkable. When my grandad passed away, you were right there by my side, offering comfort and support. I can only begin to imagine the depth of pain you have endured, losing not only your daughter but also another child. Despite the immense challenges life presented, you embraced your role as a caregiver and raised seven grandkids all on your own. Your strength has been a beacon of inspiration, showing us that we can overcome any obstacle with perseverance and love.

Your resilience is awe-inspiring. Although you never learned how to drive, you defied limitations by walking everywhere. I remember those early mornings when we would stand together, waiting for two buses to take us to school and back. No matter how cold or uncomfortable it was, you never faltered. You made a way, demonstrating that determination and resourcefulness can lead to success, even in the face of adversity.

The wisdom you imparted has been invaluable. By having us walk with you everywhere, you taught us the importance of mental fortitude and self-sufficiency. You refused rides and chose to walk, teaching us to rely on ourselves rather than depending on others or begging for assistance. Your steadfast belief in self-sufficiency has shaped our character and instilled within us a sense of resilience and determination. You taught us to ask for what we needed only once, understanding the power of self-advocacy and taking responsibility for our own lives.

Your spirituality and unwavering dedication to your faith have been a guiding light for our family. Your motto, "As long as I am able bodied, I will be about my father's business," captures the essence of your strong moral compass and commitment to living a purpose-driven life. Your faith has been a source of inspiration and a reminder of the importance of staying grounded and centered in our values.

Reflecting on our shared experiences, I am grateful for the invaluable life lessons you taught me during times of grief and challenging circumstances. Even amidst my own sorrow, you encouraged me to pursue my dreams and aspirations. Through a weekly allowance of $20, you taught me the importance of taking care of my needs and working towards my wants. This instilled in me a drive to seek more and take responsibility for my own financial well-being, which ultimately led to my first job. The lessons you imparted during those difficult times continue to guide me today, serving as a reminder of the strength and resilience we possess within ourselves.

As I journeyed through the stages of grief and embarked on the path of self-discovery, your love and wisdom provided me with the strength to accept my true self. Your unwavering support and the lessons you taught me helped me develop maturity and confidence. Today, I am able to write a new narrative for my life, one that propels me forward and embraces the guidance you provided in a way that is true to who I am.

Grandma, I am eternally grateful for the love and guidance you have bestowed upon me. Your strength, resilience, wisdom, and unwavering faith have shaped my character and continue to inspire me. Through your example, I have learned the importance of perseverance, self-sufficiency, and staying true to my values.

Thank you, Grandma, for everything you have done and continue to do. You are an extraordinary woman, and I am blessed to have you in my life.

With heartfelt appreciation,
Georgia James

Section I: Leaving for College (Separation) [ 3 Influences ]

## Chapter 1: Embracing a New Adventure

My story begins with a boy I call my first love. His name was Calvin. I say it this way because he was not my best love. That honor is reserved for my husband and forever best friend, Jerall. Let's get one thing clear right at the outset, your story has a beginning, but your story is not about where you started. Your story is what you craft and compose every day consistently showing up with your best, being the whole you without apology and ready for the context. This is true for love, life, and making a living.

**Young Enough to Know No Better**
In 8th grade, I had the pleasure of meeting Calvin. Life was a bit complicated for me back then, as I had to catch two buses just to get to school. You see, my grandmother didn't want me going to the nearby Highland Park High School, so I had to attend Winan's Academy on the East side. But it was during those bus rides that I first encountered Calvin, and little did I know, he would become my first love.

While my friends had the privilege of attending college tours with their moms, I would tag along. It was a glimpse into a world I yearned to be a part of. Determined to chase my dreams, I sought the help of a high school teacher. This teacher, whose name I unfortunately can't recall, became my guiding light. She assisted me in filling out financial aid forms and ensuring that all the necessary paperwork was in order. I would often miss buses just to sit with her and complete the paperwork, knowing that these documents held the key to my future.

But, as with any journey, obstacles arose. My grandmother accused me of sneaking around with Calvin, creating tension and making it harder for me to pursue my dreams. It was a difficult time, navigating through these challenges while also juggling the complexities of young love.

However, I believe that sometimes we are young enough to not know any better, to not fully understand the weight of the obstacles in front of us. And maybe, just maybe, that ignorance is what fuels our determination and resilience.

Despite the accusations and the doubters, Calvin and I continued to support each other and push forward. We were young and in love, but we also had dreams and aspirations that burned within us. Together, we faced the adversity with unwavering strength.

**College Playing House**

When it was time for me to go to college, my grandmother made the decision to move. She had been raising two of my cousins, and I had been the only one helping her until then. But now, with my journey to college beginning, she relocated to Ohio with her daughter and my sister in Dayton. This meant that I had to find a new place to stay until college started.

Fortunately, my brother's mom stepped in to ensure that I had a place to stay. She took me in and made sure that I had everything I needed to prepare for college. With her support, I was able to transition smoothly into this new chapter of my life.

Once college started, I found myself living in Saginaw Valley University on campus. I had roommates initially, but eventually, I moved into a single efficiency. It was during this time that someone expected started to play a significant role in my college experience - him, Calvin.

Calvin would often visit me from time to time, and he quickly grew familiar with the campus and all my friends. However, it became apparent that he didn't just want to visit occasionally. He decided to take it a step further and move into the dorm with me. This wasn't something that had been planned or discussed; it just happened.

As he became a constant presence on campus, I couldn't help but wonder about his true motives. What was his purpose for being there? Was he simply following me because he wanted to be near me? These questions lingered in my mind, but I allowed him to stay, perhaps because I was young and infatuated with the idea of having him by my side.

Days turned into weeks, and weeks turned into months. Calvin continued to linger on campus, seemingly doing nothing except being around me and my friends. It was a strange situation, as I was trying to navigate my way through college and establish my own independence, all while he remained intertwined in my university life.

Looking back, I realize that this period was a turning point in our relationship. It was a time of figuring out our boundaries and understanding what we truly wanted from each other. In many ways, it was a time of growing up and learning about the complexities of adult relationships.

In the grand scheme of things, college was about more than just playing house with someone. It was a time of self-discovery, growth, and forging our own paths. While Calvin's presence during that period certainly shaped my college experience, it was ultimately the choices I made and the lessons I learned that defined my journey.

### Old Enough to Know Better

Looking back on my college years, it's hard to imagine how foolish I was - how blinded by love and a taste of independence. One moment, I was a carefree young person, reveling in the joys of college life. The next, I was kicked off campus for smoking weed, a decision that could have easily derailed my entire future.

Calvin played a significant role in my downfall. He had introduced me to the drug, and I foolishly followed his lead without considering the consequences. In many ways, I was playing house with him, convinced that we were somehow above the law. We were risking everything for the sake of a fleeting thrill.

At that time, I was foolishly in love. I worked a few hours just to have pocket money and received loan refunds from the university. It was easy to fall into the trap of thinking we were like Bonny and Clyde, living recklessly and without regard for the possible consequences.

But then, the dorm's silent smoke alarm was triggered, and my world came crashing down. Suddenly, I realized how much I had to lose - far beyond my attachment to Calvin. The fire department showed up with the police and I foolishly took the charge on my record. I am not sure why exactly except that I did it for love. The charge forfeited my campus lease which kicked me out of the dorm. Even though I humbled myself and wrote a letter basically begging the university to allow me to stay, I was out. One of my friends eventually let me crash on their couch.

The situation was a wake-up call, but it took some time for me to fully understand its gravity. I realized that I didn't want to go back home, nor did I want to move to Ohio with my grandmother. I wanted to stay in college and continue exploring the world that had opened to me.

As time passed, many of my friends began leaving college for various reasons, including academic probation or financial issues.

But I was determined to stay, no matter the challenges I faced. Despite the setback of being kicked off campus, I fought on and eventually graduated.

Meanwhile, since Calvin's mother and uncles had moved to Nashville, he was thinking of his own reset by following them. I made the bold decision to move to Nashville without telling anyone, taking a big step towards creating a life that was truly my own...along with Calvin.

Before I left, I had to face the consequences of my actions when I went to court for the drug offense. The judge dropped the charges, as it was my first offense. Although I was grateful for this outcome, the experience left a lingering taste in my mouth, a reminder of how easy it is to make poor choices with long-lasting consequences.

**Reflections**

Looking back, I realize the importance of that journey. It wasn't just about chasing after a teenage romance; it was about fighting for the life I wanted to create for myself. It was about proving those who underestimated me wrong and showing my grandmother that I could make something of myself. Calvin was at first a pillar of support during turbulent times, and for that, I will always be grateful.

I'm grateful for the harsh lessons I learned. They taught me that love and recklessness aren't excuses for bad decisions, and that our actions have the power to impact our lives in profound ways. Through it all, I gained the resilience and determination needed to overcome challenges and build a life of purpose and fulfillment.

In the grand scheme of things, those moments on the bus and the accusations from my grandmother were just the opening chapters of my story. They were the catalysts that ignited the fire within me to strive for more. They were the beginning stages of a journey that would lead me to resilience, achievement, and self-discovery.

So here I stand today, looking back at a young girl who didn't quite know what lay ahead. A girl who faced adversity with determination and love in her heart. And as I look at the years that have passed since those bus rides, I am proud of the woman I have become, the hurdles I have overcome, and the story I have crafted for myself.

For you see, it's not just about where we start our stories, but how we navigate through life, consistently showing up with our best, unapologetically authentic, and ready for whatever challenges come our way. And this, my friend, is what I have come to realize: Our stories are not shaped solely by our beginnings, but by the choices we make every day to live with purpose, resilience, and unwavering determination.

## Chapter 2: Trouble in a Toxic Paradise

**Moving to Tennessee**

Moving to Tennessee was a decision that I made with little forethought. I didn't realize how difficult it would be to support myself, and I certainly had no idea what kind of future lay ahead of me.

When I arrived, Calvin was living out of someone's closet, and I was under the impression that he was able to support me. However, he was living with someone who was behind on their rent, and we were struggling to make ends meet. I was working full-time to pay the bills, all while attempting to keep us in the apartment. To make matters worse, my car started acting up, adding another layer of stress to an already difficult situation.

But despite the challenges we faced, Calvin soon started to betray my trust. He began cheating and taking my car without permission, leaving me feeling frustrated and alone. I was at MTSU at the time, but I soon realized that I needed to establish my independence and focus on my own growth.

Gradually, I began to recognize the importance of creating my own space and finding my own identity. Although Calvin had been an integral part of my life up until that point, we both began to realize that our paths were leading us in different directions. The college experience was molding us into individuals with unique aspirations and goals, and it was time for us to explore our own paths.

In the end, our shared memories, and the lessons we learned together remained, but our time as a couple had come to an end. I was failing all my classes at MTSU, and my guidance counselor suggested that I apply for TSU instead. It was a difficult decision, but I knew it was the right one.

That's why I didn't tell anyone I had moved to Tennessee. It wasn't that I didn't want their support, but rather that I knew I needed to make this journey on my own. It wasn't until later that I found out my grandmother had refused to sign a loan for me, instead choosing to sign for another cousin. It certainly stung, but I knew that I had to continue maturing and moving forward on my own.

**Living Dangerously in Love**

When I was living in Saginaw, my grades were excellent, and I had full confidence in my ability to succeed in college. However, it was the challenges I faced with my daily commute and the difficult home life situation that ultimately caused me to fail. Despite the setbacks, the application process for college was relatively straightforward. I didn't need to take any additional tests or remedial classes. The only hurdle I had to overcome was applying for additional funding since I was considered an out-of-state student. It presented some difficulties, but I persevered and managed to navigate through it.

My living arrangement at the time was with Calvin, who lived with someone involved in selling drugs. The problematic situation was compounded by the fact that they couldn't keep up with the rent. Essentially, it was a trap house, and the environment was far from ideal.

To make matters worse, Calvin's behavior was reckless. He would cheat on me but justified it by saying he was doing it for us. He would manipulate other girls to gain material possessions such as cars and credit cards. All I craved was love and security, but I found myself staying in the relationship due to the trauma bond we had formed. Our arguments were intense and tumultuous, but the sincerity of our makeups made it seemingly impossible to leave. However, as I gained more knowledge and maturity through my education, I became increasingly unwilling to tolerate the lifestyle Calvin embraced.

Eventually, things reached a breaking point, and Calvin and I got into a heated fight. In a fit of anger, he put me out of our shared living space. There I stood outside, overwhelmed with emotions, tears streaming down my face.

This moment became a turning point for me. It made me realize that I needed to prioritize my own stability and well-being. As painful as it was, it became clear that I couldn't continue down this path with Calvin. I needed to shift my focus back to my education and myself.

In the midst of the chaos and heartache, I made the decision to move forward. The journey ahead seemed daunting, but I was determined to rise above these challenges and create a better future for myself. I knew that I had the strength and resilience to overcome the obstacles that lay ahead, and I was ready to embark on a new chapter of my life.

That's not to say that I was strong enough to leave Calvin altogether.

During this tumultuous time, I happened to befriend one of Calvin's customers named Justin. Justin had previously bought weed from Calvin and saw that I had been put out of our shared living space. He took compassion on me and extended an invitation to live with him.

Justin and I quickly developed a strong friendship, and he was staying with a lady at the time. Eventually, we decided to find our own place together, solidifying our bond. Through Justin, I also became acquainted with his friends who became my friends as well. One of his friends happened to be skilled at fixing cars, while another was a hairstylist, catering to Justin's personal style.

Despite attending Tennessee State University (TSU), I wasn't actively involved in the social scene. I had already experienced that in Saginaw, and everything I did, I did with Justin by my side.

Despite feeling hurt and betrayed by Calvin, as well as dealing with the deterioration of our relationship and my struggles with school, I accepted Justin's offer. However, deep down, I was deeply disappointed that my family remained unaware of the situation I was facing.

I continued to go to work and financially contribute to our living situation as I could. At times, I would find myself running out of gas and fabricating stories about losing my debit card in order to receive money through MoneyGram for gas.

I was still involved with Calvin. He knew that he had a hold on me. He was aware that he could always lure me back into his life. This power dynamic allowed him to mistreat me, while still enjoying the benefits of our relationship. It's worth mentioning that Calvin's mom did not approve of me and held a negative opinion towards me.

Justin, however, wasn't willing to tolerate Calvin's presence. He firmly prohibited him from coming over to our new place. Despite Justin's wishes, I would occasionally sneak Calvin in. Justin would rightfully call me out on my actions, expressing his frustration and anger at my seemingly foolish choices. At one point, I even contemplated having a baby with Calvin, something I am now grateful never came to fruition. Unfortunately, I found myself feeling trapped in this unhealthy and toxic cycle.

This period in my life was characterized by complexity and internal turmoil. The bonds I formed with individuals like Justin offered me some solace, but the ongoing connection and manipulation from Calvin kept me suspended in a state of uncertainty. Little did I know that a major shift was about to occur that would prompt me to reassess my priorities and make decisions that would eventually lead me towards personal growth and liberation.

### Liberation through a Prison Sentence

After reaching my breaking point and experiencing various hardships, I finally made the decision to move out on my own.

Not long after, the situation with Calvin took a turn for the worse. The police started actively looking for him, and he became a sought-after target. Eventually, he ended up in jail, and I found myself putting money on his books to support him during his year-long incarceration. I was constantly worried about his safety and well-being, as my mind was consumed by my love for him.

During the time we were together, Calvin was involved in selling weed and pills. While my main concern was his safety, he would often take advantage of me and use my car for his dealings. I would overlook these actions, simply grateful for the thought that he was coming back to me. He would make some money from his sales and selfishly keep it all for himself. He even attempted to convince me to hand over my school refund checks so he could use them to make a profit, but I always resisted, refusing to allow him to exploit me in that way. This was the unfortunate reality of the life I had become accustomed to.

As time went on, my house began to resemble a trap house in that there were always people coming and going. The constant presence of strangers in my home only added to the sense of chaos and instability in my life.

One day, after returning home from work, I was met with murmurs from the people in my neighborhood. They recounted the events of a raid that had taken place. Apparently, Calvin had run through the house in an attempt to evade the police. The news spread quickly, and I heard whispers of "C-Note just got locked up." The story included details of the police forcefully breaking down doors and chasing after him, leaving behind a trail of chaos and uncertainty.

This event was yet another shocking reminder of the destructive path that Calvin had led me down. It solidified my decision to distance myself from him and focus on rebuilding my own life and finding a way out of the turbulent existence I had found myself in.

### Meeting My First Mentor: Mr. Right

During this tumultuous time in my life, fate led me to meet Jerall, who would eventually become my first mentor. It was a chance encounter while I was working at a gas station and taking my dog for a walk by the lake. Jerall walked by a few times, and eventually struck up a conversation with me, asking if I wanted to exchange numbers.

At that time, I was still holding onto the hope that things would work out with Calvin. So, unaware of Jerall's true intentions, I saw him only as an option and quickly gave him my number, anticipating using his truck to visit Calvin.

Despite the complicated dynamic with Calvin, Jerall persisted in showing me care and support. He proved to be a kind and generous individual who had his life together and wasn't taking advantage of me like Calvin had been. In fact, he even bought my books for one semester, which was a pivotal moment that made me see him in a new light.

However, my situation became even more complicated when I discovered that I was pregnant, and Calvin found out about Jerall. His release from prison in 2011 left me feeling conflicted about what to do next.

As events unfolded, Calvin's hold on me slowly dissipated and I found myself gravitating more towards Jerall. But the struggle continued, as I found myself dealing with Calvin's death in November 2012, just months before the birth of my daughter with Jerall, Harmony, in May of that same year. The challenging circumstances of my life had created a complicated web of emotions and relationships that would take time and effort to unravel. In the midst of all this, Jerall's support and guidance would prove to be invaluable in helping me to find a sense of stability and purpose in my life.

It's both wise and frustrating to realize that there are certain experiences that daughters will inevitably go through. As a mother, I hope to instill in my own daughters the importance of finding happiness within themselves, so that they won't feel the need to rely on men for their sense of fulfilment. Reflecting on my own journey, I understand that falling in love and relying on a man was something I couldn't shield them from. My only hope is that the love and support they receive from their father and me will help them navigate through it more quickly.

It may sound strange, but being around a certain group of people helped me see myself in a different light. They saw past the broken little orphan girl persona that I had carried with me, and I began to see it too. Their perspective started to influence and inspire me. Gradually, when I returned home, people noticed a change in me. Their doubts about my capabilities seemed to melt away as they witnessed me making progress. At the time, I wasn't aware of the impact I was having, but it was clear that I was authentically being myself and it was resonating with others.

Throughout this period of growth, I never stopped pursuing my education. I had a strong desire to create a better financial future for myself and my family, and I aspired to become a social worker. Unlike many of my peers, I wasn't invested in the party scene. While I did partake in some activities, I knew that I had something more to offer the world. Moving to Tennessee wasn't just about seeking fun; it was a step towards achieving my goals and making a meaningful impact.

If there's one piece of advice I could offer to anyone, it would be to embrace your authentic self. Stay true to who you are and let that guide your actions and decisions. It may not always be easy, but being genuine and staying focused on your aspirations will help you make progress and move towards your goals.

## Chapter 3: Seeing Me for the First Time

As I walked into Tennessee State University (TSU) as a freshman, I felt a wave of excitement wash over me. I was eager to start this new chapter in my life and gain knowledge that would help me excel in my future career. However, my excitement was short-lived as I realized how lost and alone I felt in this new environment. I was struggling to adapt to this new space, and I was overwhelmed by the high expectations that were set upon me.

**The Mentor Dr. Right**
One day, I found myself sitting in Dr. Michael A. Wright's classroom. At that point, I had already sat in a few different classes, but I distinctly remember sitting in his class and feeling a completely different energy. Being from Pontiac, not far from my birthplace of Detroit, Dr. Wright and I had something of a shared experience. Whenever I wrote stories or completed assignments, I tried to make them personal. Dr. Wright was always able to see that and bring them to life, whether it was something I looked at or the narrative itself.

During one particular class, I remember him talking about changing the narrative of our lives. He explained that we did not have to be the person we had always thought ourselves to be. That we could change our narrative and be whatever we wanted to be. I felt something changing right away. As I sat there and listened to him talk, I began to see my past as fluid and a past that I could shape into any future I desired. Suddenly, it was as if a switch had been flipped inside of me.

That prior year in particular was extremely difficult for me. I had struggled with self-esteem and self-worth in the past pushing through without the parents I loved, lost, and missed dearly. Growing up in Detroit, I had faced several challenges that affected my confidence. I was used to constantly questioning myself and my potential. That's just how it was in my family. However, after listening to Dr. Wright, I realized that I could change the narrative of my life. It suddenly dawned on me that I did not have to be held back by my past experiences. I could be whoever I wanted to be.

Dr. Wright's class became a revelation for me. His words opened a whole new world of possibilities. I began to feel like I had a purpose and direction for my life. I started to work with expectation. I began to gain more confidence in myself. I took his words and used them as a mantra of sorts, repeating them to myself whenever self-doubt started to creep in.

Looking back, I realize how lucky I was to have Dr. Wright as my professor. His words and encouragement were exactly what I needed to hear at that time in my life. He helped me see that I was capable of so much more than I had ever thought possible. I will forever be grateful for his influence in my life and for teaching me how to change the narrative of my life.

Yeah, it felt like a divine intervention. I tell people every chance I get. Dr. Wright was the first person in my life who truly believed in me. He saw me for who I am today, even back when I was just a student in his classroom, struggling with assignments and reaching out in tears. He saw potential in me that no one else did. Others saw a silly girl who had lost her parents and couldn't do anything on her own. But he saw beyond that.

His belief in me has shaped my confidence. I used to struggle to trust my own abilities and capabilities. I think it stems from my childhood when there were no cheerleaders to tell me I could do anything, no one to say I was great. Instead, there were voices cautioning me against aiming too high, admonishing me not to pursue big dreams. Maybe they had good intentions, but it hindered my ability to believe in myself.

That's why it's so crucial to have someone who believes in you. When you have someone like that, you don't want to let them down. But it's more than that. You start questioning what they see in you because you don't see it yourself. So you go searching, trying to discover what they're seeing. And in that search, you begin to find confidence because if they believe in you, maybe there's something worth believing in. You may not fully understand it, but you trust them enough to give it a try.

Dr. Wright once told me, "You need to have someone who believes in you because most of us don't want to disappoint that belief. But it's not just about disappointing them, it's about asking ourselves, 'What do they see in me? What am I missing?' And in that pursuit, you find the confidence to try, even if you don't fully see what they see for yourself."

Dr. Wright became my greatest mentor. My mentor was able to see me and my future success when others could not. I know how much power it holds when someone can see something beautiful within you when you are uncertain. I felt those things within me. I knew I could do better. Having someone who believed in me and articulated it, made me know that I was not crazy. The people that knew me and should have known me were negative and limiting. I began to let them go. I realized that I was growing beyond the experience and potential of my trauma and my small town. As I began to understand that I would strive harder. It wasn't that they did not believe in me. They were scared because it had never been done before. They assumed that I would not be able to do it because they were uncertain about their ability.

## The Butler

I had some difficulties with other teachers in the social work program. One of them was Ms. Butler. It felt like she intentionally made things difficult for me for unknown reasons. In contrast, Dr. Wright didn't give me such a hard time. It seemed like Miss Butler made everything more complicated than it needed to be. I often felt judged by her, as if she believed I would never amount to anything or take anything seriously.

As I continued attending her classes and getting to know her more, my perspective of Miss Butler changed. Even on the last day, during our big presentation, she left a distasteful impression on me. She always appeared judgmental and wore a face of disapproval.

From other students, it became clear that Ms. Butler had a reputation for being judgmental, cruel, and harsh. However, I noticed that some students had given her the opportunity to complain about them by not completing assignments, submitting homework late, or being unprepared. Dr. Wright never spoke ill of Ms. Butler. He always encouraged students to be better than those who accused, challenged, or irritated them. He offered support and cheerleading and held them accountable for their actions.

Some students eventually acknowledged the purpose behind Ms. Butler's approach. Some even expressed some appreciation. They realized that she was tough on them to prepare them for the challenges they may face in life. I still think her methods are not ideal, but I know I can overcome difficult situations because of the resilience they developed under her guidance.

Overall, the initial frustration and judgment I experienced with Ms. Butler has shifted to a recognition of the lessons she was trying to impart. I now understand that her intentions were rooted in preparing us for the hardships of the real world. She didn't have to do it the way she did it. She could have done it a different way. She didn't have to make me feel bad about myself. She could have supported me more directly and intentionally instead of making me figure it out. Sure, I should be expected to prepare and figure out the assignment, but I shouldn't have to figure out my whole developmental struggle. That's the difference with Dr. Wright. He helped me understand the developmental struggle of my life and how I could construct something better. From that position, I could recognize where I was making poor choices and make different ones. I could own my response to even the venom of Ms. Butler and feel good about myself regardless of external messages.

Despite the distasteful memories, I appreciate the resilience and determination it instilled in me and my fellow students. I also know that growth was my choice in a less-than-ideal situation. As a practitioner, I take a more constructive approach with my clients—more like Dr. Wright.

**The Motivation**

First, my motivation was just about finishing school. My biggest fear was that I wouldn't finish. There were moments when it seemed like I could get stuck not having the finances, the time, the foundational knowledge. So, of course, I went out and got pregnant! I was afraid of the danger that pregnancy might bring. At that moment, I was worried that it could turn into one of those situations that limit a life.

I felt ashamed and embarrassed because I felt like I was doing exactly what my family expected me to do. They said I would come down here and get ready, and then I would drop out of school. In my mind, I thought, "Oh my God, I'm proving them right." During that time, I had this strong desire to prove them wrong. It wasn't just about what I wanted to do; it was also fueled by this need to show them that they were mistaken. Unfortunately, that's when I got pregnant with Harvey. That's when the fight to prove them wrong intensified, because now it was like, "Okay, you said this would happen, and look, it did. I got pregnant."

So that was my biggest battle - proving people wrong and showing them that I could do it. But I also hid my pregnancy. I would always wear big shirts and coats to hide my stomach because I felt ashamed and embarrassed.

One day in April, I finally admitted it to myself and revealed it to the one person I did not want to disappoint, Dr. Wright. It was my first time sharing the news with someone. I still remember how disappointed he looked. He voiced his reservations and then seemed to adopt a different perspective. "What's done is done. Now, we make the most of it." He promised to be present for me. I promised I would finish. Then, to the pregnancy.

The way it happened was quite unexpected and crazy. I didn't find out I was pregnant until March, and I was in denial. I didn't tell my family until April because I was about to visit them in Ohio. So when I finally told them, they thought I was probably two or three months pregnant. I suspected I might be pregnant in March, around my birthday, because I was trying to drink and smoke. Jarrell told me I should go to the doctor and confirm if I was pregnant first. In my mind, I was in denial and believed I was only two or three months pregnant. But in reality, I was already nine months along because I gave birth to Harmony the next month.

When I went to the doctor, they did all the necessary tests and confirmed my pregnancy. I hadn't been taking any prenatal pills or vitamins because I didn't have any insurance. The doctors couldn't do much without insurance due to liability concerns. So I didn't receive proper prenatal care or ultrasounds. I had to apply for state insurance, and it was only at the end of April, after everything got approved and I finally had insurance, that I could go for my first doctor's appointment. Since I didn't have insurance, I had to handle my own prenatal care. I went to a place called Lintz Health Department, and they provided me with prenatal vitamins.

I wasn't prepared for her arrival. Jarrell had just started a new job, and he had been unemployed the entire time. Meanwhile, I was working two jobs and attending school. We were living in my apartment in Hermitage at that time. I would go to school in the morning and work at night. I continued working right up until I had Harmony. Oh, and where were you working? I had two jobs at the time - one at the gas station and another at Kroger's.

On the night I was supposed to work, I began experiencing intense contractions. However, I didn't think I was in labor because they had told me I wasn't due until June. It was probably around May 21st, and I was preparing to go to work that night.

I gave birth to Harmony on May 22nd. On the day Harmony was born, we were in the hospital when they called Jarrell to inform him that he had gotten the job. It was quite a coincidence. It felt like a miracle.

## Chapter 4: New Beginnings and Responsibilities

Harmony's personality keeps me grounded. Well, that's why she behaves the way she does with me. When she was younger, I'm not sure how she acts now. But yeah, I'm a Gemini. That's cool. So, how did she change? How did having her change your outlook on things, if at all?

Having Harmony definitely had a significant impact on me. It was really tough. I was still going to school and only getting paid $9-11 an hour, without any state assistance because they wanted me to put Jarrell on child support. That was the only way I could receive any state aid. So, I had to continue trying to make ends meet, oftentimes falling short. It was difficult, especially during Christmas or her birthday. I would cry because I felt like I could only provide the basics for my baby.

There were times when Dr. Wright and his wife would give me a bag of things for her, and it meant so much to me. It was like Christmas to us because we were really struggling. Every time that happened, I would cry because I felt like it was my fight and hers as well. I felt like I owed her a better life.

I knew that finishing school and pursuing my dreams would enable me to provide a better life for her. At the time, I was working odd jobs and often bringing her to class with me since I didn't have much family support. Your mother didn't help watch Harmony because she didn't believe that Jerell was her father, so that made things even more challenging. I used to take Harmony to class with me, and it made me determined to finish my education. Many people doubted me, especially my family, who didn't think I could take care of a baby here without much family support.

**Good Annoying Harmony**

Harmony has always been so vibrant. I say she can be annoying, but it's a happy kind of annoying. It's like she's still in that phase where she enjoys doing childlike things. It makes sense because, at the time of this writing, she's eleven. She always wants to have picnics, watch movies, or do other activities together. No matter how tired I am, she will say, "Mama, let's have a picnic. Me, you, and the dog." It's always just me and her. She has a hard time sharing and her world revolves around me. Even when she gives Jerell a birthday card or anything, she writes in his card, "I love my mommy!"

Her world is centered around her mama. And if she feels something is wrong with me, she asks, "Mama, what do you want? Do you want me to quit this job? Mama, what's wrong? Let's go play with the dog. Let's have a picnic." It's funny because you would think she has outgrown these things, but she still wants to do them. The other kids don't want to, but she still wants to have family nights, watch movies, have snacks, and play games.

It makes me realize how much I have changed because these were activities I used to do with her. Now, my career has taken me to a different level and I'm often too exhausted to participate. She loves those things because of our past experiences. We used to have movie nights, go on picnics, play with the dogs. I just don't want to do it anymore because work drains me. Sometimes it takes a lot for me to want to do anything because I just want to stay home and relax. Harmony even jokes that if she could go back in my uterus, she would.

But she doesn't get upset about my absences. She does have her moments of only child syndrome, but she is mostly always happy, vibrant, and full of energy. She still enjoys doing those family things while her older siblings close themselves behind the doors of their rooms.

**New Purpose**

When I was in school, people thought I was going to drop out, but I was determined to prove them wrong. I wanted it so badly that I stopped caring about anyone else's thoughts. It became personal, and I was set on becoming a social worker no matter what. Harmony played a big role in keeping me motivated. She was so vibrant and had so much of me and her together that it fueled me to keep going. Even on bad days with Jerall, I knew that Harmony loved me unconditionally. My purpose changed. I was no longer doing this to prove anyone wrong. I was doing it to provide a better life for Harmony.

I had jobs that allowed me to bring her to work with me. Even Waffle House allowed me to bring her with me. I have always had jobs that would allow me to keep her. Dr. Wright would engage Harmony while I was in his classes. The only problem was Ms. Butler's classes.

I used to take her to a daycare while I attended Miss Butler's class. One day, I brought her to class with me, and Miss Butler made me take her out because she considered it a liability to have her in the classroom. I had a test to take in that class, and I didn't have anyone to watch Harmony.

I owed the daycare $100 and was afraid that they would not accept a drop-off. I prayed all the way to the daycare. I was nervous they would notice that I owed them money, but they didn't seem to pay attention. They allowed me to drop her off without incident. It was moments like these that were difficult, but I did what I had to do to keep moving forward.

I jokingly say Harmony is annoying, but it doesn't truly feel that way to me. It feels more like I'm overworked and lacking the energy to do the things I used to enjoy. It's like everything has changed. So, it's really important for me to figure this out. We all must find a balance in our lives.

I realize that I can't play all day, but I also don't want to let these years slip away without appreciating the time I have with my daughter. I know she wants to spend time with me and have picnics, but she's growing up so fast. She's outgrowing the little cars and toys she used to love.

So, I need to acknowledge this phase of her life and make the effort to spend quality time with her in different ways. It's a challenge, but I'm working on it. And I'm glad for that. This is an important chapter in my life, and I know it will teach me valuable lessons for the future.

**Believing in Me**

I believe in me because it's the truth. And you know what's funny? I am truly awesome. It's not like I'm making up anything to boost my self-esteem. The brilliance within me is undeniable, and I've come to embrace it. Sure, there are times when I don't fully understand all of it, and that's perfectly fine.

You don't have to fully comprehend it either. Just know that I see it within myself. So I keep pushing forward, regardless of any setbacks or challenges. That's what I tell people in my life right now. That's all there is to it. This job can't bring me down because even if they fired me tomorrow, I'd find a way to figure it out. They don't have power over me.

If I listened to the naysayers, I shouldn't even be here. If I listened to my family or worried about what others have gone through, I would not have a degree. I would never have moved or started college. Calvin ended up in jail, and he's no longer with us. But here I am, defying all expectations, moving on to the next level. That's just the way it is because I'm the one in control.

My influence isn't just limited to my role as a counselor or when I connect with others. It all starts at home when I support my daughter and the two other children I've adopted. I am the greatest influence on their lives, and I'm constantly finding ways to make it work.

The cool thing is, it gets even better when you start to figure it out. You begin to understand how to relax and let things unfold, despite the fact that people may still do you wrong. They may overwork you, overlook your work, or even steal it. But once you realize that these things aren't in your control, you can finally let go and find some peace.

The message that has been clear to me, and that I want to pass on to you, is the importance of being absolutely clear about what you want from life. If your desire is to continue working in a group home with adults, then you need to have a clear understanding of what that entails and be unwavering in your commitment.

However, it's crucial to take a step back and reevaluate if that is still what you truly want. That's what I wanted while I was in school. Now, my focus has shifted towards spending quality time with my daughter, raising her, and nurturing my relationship with Jarrell. Not everyone wants to work incessantly, and that's okay. Freedom is more valuable to me than obtaining other things, although I do recognize their value and importance.

It's essential to identify what brings you happiness and what you are striving for. The universe will respond by providing opportunities that you cannot create on your own or may not even be aware of. However, you must gain absolute clarity on what you truly want. For instance, if a group home with adults is your ultimate goal, be mindful of the amount of work and time it requires to build from scratch and manage employees.

Consider whether you truly desire that path. It can be overwhelming, and it's essential to reassess your priorities. The universe will guide you, helping you realize that maybe it's not what you truly want. It's a way of training you to understand your own desires. You may want to care for people, consult with them, or pursue something entirely different. Once you define your true desires, the universe will support you in those specific ways.

It's important to reflect on these lessons and make decisions that align with our true goals and desires.

**What I Want**

I really don't enjoy being stressed out. Taking life too seriously has never been my thing. I learned at a young age how short life can be, especially after losing some important people in my life. So, I prefer to take things lightly and have fun.

Although it can still be challenging at times, I find myself drawn to the things I've been told not to do. I want to go back to the days when I played with my dog, had picnics, and didn't feel irritable or agitated. For me, that means getting up, going to the park, working out, eating healthily, drinking water, and simply doing what I want throughout the day.

I don't want anyone stressing me out or constantly calling and bothering me. I'm still making money, doing therapy on the side, and I have other things going on that I enjoy. I'm comfortable and not living paycheck to paycheck. I have my life insurance, health insurance, and savings accounts in order. I've got everything sorted out.

I don't feel the need to have it all because I don't need the newest car or the latest stuff. I just want to be happy. I want to laugh and play, have moments of seriousness, but ultimately enjoy life without constantly stressing over bills or worrying about the news.

I don't want to deal with difficult people and their attitudes. I'm tired of having to prove myself to those who can't see me for who I truly am. I shouldn't have to get upset or think of ways to confront them and use harsh words. I might not always know how to respond professionally through email, but trust me, I know how to handle those situations.

But honestly, I just don't want to deal with all that. I wish people could just do right and treat others with respect. Why do some people have to resort to bullying or taking advantage of others? And then have the audacity to ask why I want more money? It's because I don't want to deal with people like that. Like my sister says, I live in this crazy LA world, you know?

So, yeah, that's about it. I know I've said a lot, but ultimately, everything else fades away when I focus on finding happiness. I don't want to keep feeling overwhelmed and underappreciated.

I want to build my own counseling practice, have flexible hours, and earn a good income. This way, I can organize my time the way I want it and truly live life on my terms.

I'm not going to treat my daughter like she's in second place. I won't snap at my husband or anyone else for that matter. I've realized that it's up to me to choose my responses. I'm not going to snap at anybody. I've decided not to worry about it. It's not giving up; it's recognizing that if you all aren't going to give me what I need, I'm not going to exhaust myself to keep you comfortable. I refuse to sacrifice my well-being to appease you.

So, I'm going to prioritize taking care of myself. I'm going to take care of the people I love. And if you don't like the way I'm doing that and want to fire me, okay. I'll simply apply for unemployment. I won't stress over you all, but I certainly won't let you dictate my mood or how I interact with people. I won't allow you to take away my movie night.

I won't let you make my daughter wish I quit either. No, that's not even an option anymore. I'll leave work on time, and I'll leave all your nonsense behind. That's what I'm giving up on, trying to make people do the right thing and trying to fix their situations. No, that's not my responsibility. Your situation can be different. That's why you'll write it down, because your situation is unique.

It's not giving up on the idea of a group home, but rather adapting to new information. It's growing and realizing that what I thought I wanted was driven by trying to take care of my grandma and others. I do enjoy helping people, but now I know that specific path is too stressful and won't bring me the fulfillment I desire. There are just too many people I must please.

Now what? I don't know that yet. Now, what I do know is that I find therapy enjoyable. I thrive in one-on-one interactions and perhaps even group interactions with people. I'm going to pursue it in a different way. I'll do it in a way that allows me to go home afterward without worrying about your destructive behavior or whether you received your medications. That's not my job or responsibility. It's called evolution, and I'm proud of myself for growing and making these decisions.

## Section II: Loss of Grandfather, Mother, and Father (Descent) [ 3 Losses ]

## Chapter 5: GRACE - Strength amid Struggles

**Highland Park Upbringing**

Growing up in Highland Park, Michigan was a challenging yet rewarding experience. My grandparents served as my primary caregivers, and they held very traditional beliefs, especially my grandmother. Despite the difficulties, the memories I have from that time are vivid and sweet. Our home was located on Ford Street, which meant that nothing was kept a secret. As kids, we were aware of everything that was happening around us, even if we didn't fully understand it.

Living in a neighborhood plagued by drug problems had its own set of consequences. Some of our family members were either involved in selling drugs or were users themselves. Witnessing this firsthand was truly frightening. However, because we were related to these individuals, it was an accepted reality that we had to navigate.

I can still recall interacting with the crack addicts on our block as a child. It may seem strange, but it was a normal part of our lives. Highland Park was a close-knit community, and everyone seemed to know our family. Our parents had gone to school with these individuals, and now we were going to school with their children. Despite their struggles, the addicts were often kind to us, assisting our grandmother with household chores or accompanying us to the store. As children, we would sometimes laugh at their peculiar behavior, not fully comprehending the extent of their addiction.

Despite the hardships, we loved playing outside as kids. Our neighborhood didn't stop us from riding bikes, playing games like cops and robbers and red-light-green-light, or shooting hoops. Even a trip to the corner store to buy chips and candy brought us joy. And, of course, the ice cream truck was always a highlight of our day.

However, these childhood memories were often interrupted by the sound of gunshots. It seemed that every day, around the same time, we would find ourselves rushing through our neighbor's back door to avoid getting caught in the crossfire. I will never forget one day when I was eight years old and witnessed a drive-by shooting while standing on the sidewalk. My mother was on the porch, screaming in fear for my safety. The shooter, amidst the chaos, hollered at me to get down. It was an unforgettable moment that reminded me of the frequent violence we had grown accustomed to. Even our grandparents had become desensitized to it.

Growing up in Highland Park, Michigan was far from easy. It exposed me to the harsh realities of drugs and violence at a young age. However, it also instilled in me a sense of resilience and a deep appreciation for the small joys that life had to offer. Despite the challenges, there were moments of sweetness and connection that I will forever cherish.

### A Grandfather's Last Moments

I have always seen my grandmother as the pillar of our family, but growing up, I felt a closer connection with my grandfather. He was the one who took on the responsibility of transportation since my grandmother never learned to drive. One particular day, January 23, 1995, stands out vividly in my memory as it changed our lives forever.

My grandfather had a single-seater truck, and that day my grandmother went into a store to pick up her medicine. I was resting my head on my grandfather's shoulder when he suddenly pushed me off, something he had never done before. Confused and startled, I looked up to see him drooling with wide, red eyes. Panic set in, and I wanted to get out of the truck immediately.

As my grandmother returned, she too became alarmed, unsure of what was happening to her husband. In that moment, my grandfather took his final breath and unknowingly shifted the truck into drive, propelling us straight into oncoming traffic. I glanced up to my left and saw my unconscious grandfather. The devastation of the moment was overwhelming, and I struggled to comprehend what had just transpired. To add to the tragedy, it all occurred on my mother's birthday, turning what should have been a day of celebration into unimaginable sorrow.

To honor my grandfather's wishes, our family decided to bury him in Louisiana, his home state. We rented two vans to transport everyone from Detroit to Louisiana for his funeral. In one of the vans, I traveled with my mother, aunt, and uncle. I slept for most of the journey, only to wake up to chaos I could hardly comprehend. Helicopters hovered overhead, sirens blared, there was snow on the ground, fire, and countless people trying to free me from my seatbelt.

Filled with panic, I managed to unbuckle myself and crawled out onto the cold snow. The scene before me was a nightmare—my mother trapped under the van, surrounded by shattered glass and blood. People rushed to my side, trying to comfort me amid the chaos. I was scared speechless, hoping desperately that it was all just a bad dream.

Finally, I was able to see my mother and grandmother, and it nearly broke me. Seeing my mother sprawled on a table was terrifying, and my grandmother's face was disfigured. Her nose was in the wrong place, and her mouth and eyes had shards of glass in them. Mentally, I didn't think I would be able to cope. I wanted to ask God "why" but questioning God wasn't an option. Our neighbors, who were close to our family, had to come and get me because my family spent months in the hospital.

The events that unfolded brought about drastic changes within my family. It was incredibly difficult to carry on without my grandfather. I rarely saw my mother, and in those moments when she was present, I clung to her, crying and feeling angry that she had to leave. I couldn't understand why she wouldn't take me with her or where she would go. I had so many unanswered questions that weighed heavily on my young mind. At times, I would go to her house and have my own room, but the inconsistency made it difficult to adjust, so I always ended up back at my grandmother's house.

**Losing My Father**

My school days were tough; I was an average student and faced bullying from other kids. But one day, May 25, 1998, was surprisingly different. I couldn't believe how good the day was going. The teachers were kind, and even my peers were acting friendly. I wondered why I was having such a great day, but I dismissed the thought and simply enjoyed the moment.

When I arrived home, exhaustion overwhelmed me, and I fell into a deep sleep. I remember my aunt waking me up, urging me to go upstairs to my room. Waking up from my nap, I wished I could have stayed asleep. As I made my way downstairs, I saw my mother sitting on the couch, surrounded by my grandmother and a few other people. They guided me to sit at the table with our next-door neighbor, whom we called granddad because we were so close to their family. All I remember of him saying to me was, "Gege, do you know where your granddad is?" I replied with a hesitant "Yes." He continued, "Well, that's where your daddy is now, in heaven." At that moment, I understood that going to heaven meant dying. And like a baby, I began to cry. While I didn't live with my father, I knew him. I remembered him coming around, picking me up, and taking me to his house and other places. Most importantly, he always called me his little princess.

On every birthday, without fail, he would call and sing "Happy Birthday" to me, channeling his inner Stevie Wonder. In that moment, it felt like everyone and everything I loved was going to die, and I couldn't help but wonder who might be next.

**Losing My Mother**

Life had taken a toll on me, and I feared losing everyone close to me. Death had entered my life, and it terrified me. My grandmother and I had become extremely close, and I loved her strength and the love she had for me. I could always tell that she was worried for me, but she never left my side through all those difficult times. To cope with the pain, she kept me close to the church and tried to talk about the situation. However, I never wanted to discuss it because it only made me sad and depressed.

One of my mother's closest friends, whom we affectionately called Auntie Pat, was always there for me. She loved me like her own child and was willing to do anything for me. Just thinking about her brings tears to my heart and soul. She was also my rock, and I recall instances where my grandma would say no, but then I would go behind her back, and Auntie Pat would say yes. Those were the days.

On August 10, 1999, I was downstairs eating watermelon while my grandmother was upstairs when the phone rang. It was my mother wanting to speak to me. I hadn't seen or talked to her in weeks, so it was great to hear her voice and I couldn't wait for her to come over to Grandma's house. After speaking with my cousin and me, we disconnected. I was still downstairs watching television and eating my watermelon when the phone rang again ten minutes later. I answered, but my grandma was already on the phone. I could hear my mother's neighbor screaming and shouting, "Niece just passed out," and all I could hear was screaming. I immediately hung up the phone and tried my best to stay calm. But my grandmother rushed downstairs and told me to go next door.

As I rushed out the door, my heart was pounding so loud that I could barely hear my grandma's voice behind me. Everything went so quickly; I imagined seeing the and the neighbors gathering around. In my mind, I pushed through the crowd to see my mother lying on the ground with paramedics administering emergency treatment. Before I could reach her, I saw the light in her eyes fade, and soon she was gone. Just like that.

I could hardly believe it. My mother had called me just before she passed, but that was no comfort. The thoughts of her once living and now were not too much for me to bear. Death had taken her, and it frightened me to think that death could take anyone, at any time, without warning.

The grief that followed was overwhelming. It was as if my heart had shattered into a million pieces, and nothing could put it back together. I didn't want to leave my house, didn't want to eat, and didn't want to talk to anyone. How could I? My mother was gone, and it seemed impossible to move on without her. The fear of death and the pain associated with it had now become a part of me, one that I could not shake. It was a pain that gripped so tightly I never thought it would loosen its hold.

## Chapter 6: RESILIENCE - Contemplating the Path Forward

It's no longer a daily question, but at least weekly I contemplate my path forward amidst grief. I come to terms with my family's background and how it has shaped me, while realizing that my aspirations have led me in a different direction. Through self-reflection, I acknowledge that while my circumstances may have been challenging, I have the power to work for what I want and to shape my own destiny. It is through this journey of personal growth and maturity that I am slowly overcoming the blame I once placed on my parents and embracing the power to create my own future.

**Tempted to Quit College**
During my college years, there was a point when I seriously considered quitting. When I started my Master's degree, I would constantly reach out to my mentor for help with every single assignment. It had been a while since I graduated from my undergraduate program, so I felt lost and unsure.

I can't quite put it into words, but one day, something clicked for me. I realized that I wasn't trusting in my own capabilities. I automatically assumed that I wouldn't be able to understand the coursework.

As I embarked on my Master of Social Work program, I was filled with uncertainty and confusion. Week after week, I would call Dr. Wright, practically begging him to explain assignments using language that I could comprehend. Then, at some point, something happened that he had always predicted. I just stopped reaching out for help.

What happened? It finally clicked for me. That's how it felt. In the beginning, I would almost constantly text and ask for guidance on every assignment. But then, it felt like everything fell into place. I began to manage the workload and started comprehending the assignments. It had been such a long time since I was in school, so I was initially overwhelmed during those first few weeks. I would send you assignments, asking you to break them down for me because I couldn't understand them at first. But after a while, I got into the groove of things, realizing that the Master's program was something I was fully engaged in.

You know, I started to get the hang of it. It's hard to explain, but it was like I suddenly understood the assignments. I was fully invested and felt like I finally grasped it. Initially, I doubted my own capabilities and didn't think I would be able to comprehend it. But as I delved deeper into this field of work, something clicked and I found a rhythm. That's when I stopped reaching out for help from Dr. Wright because I felt confident that I could handle it on my own. I began to engage the professors and my classmates feeling I could ask intelligent questions and comprehend their answers. I started to understand the content, the theory, and the practice. And when I started receiving feedback on my assignments and building relationships with the professors, at least the ones who were recurring, it was like a confirmation that I got it.

Yes, I often find myself in situations where I have to remind myself of my worth. I'll have moments where I question if I have what it takes. But then I'll think about the book I wrote, the degree I earned, and the licensure I'm working towards. I remind myself that I am accomplishing things that others may not understand or haven't achieved themselves. It's important for me to remember that people see me for who I am now, not the broken little girl I once was. So, even in new and uncomfortable situations, I try to let go of old insecurities and focus on what I have accomplished.

So, it's really empowering for me to say that I have experience in various capacities of social work. There's a lot to consider, like different diagnoses and assessing situations from different angles. It's important not to let others make you doubt yourself when you know what you're talking about.

And you know, when I look back on my book, it gives me so much confidence. I mean, writing a book is a big accomplishment. It reminds me of who I am. I've worked in a group home, navigating challenging situations and having important conversations with people. It's a far cry from my past experiences working in fast food restaurants. Sometimes, I used to look at you and think, "Will I ever be able to talk and carry myself like that?" You always seemed so amazing in your fancy suits, with your hair and nails perfectly done. I always desired to have that professional presence.

And now, when you look at me, I say, "Bitch, you run this!" I run four group homes, and people answer to me. My phone rings all day with calls of "Miss Georgia, Miss Georgia." I'm doing therapy, something I've always wanted to do. So I constantly remind myself of who I am, and it gives me the confidence that I sometimes feel like I lack, but in reality, I possess it.

**Like Me or Not I'm Here**

It's something I must remind myself of every day. Whether it's addressing a situation with an employee or feeling defeated because I'm tired of discussing certain matters, I must take a step back and evaluate the situation. I say to myself, "You know what? At the end of the day, I'm the boss. I'm running this show. If you want to comply with what I say, that's fine. If not, that's your choice. I'm not here for you to like me."

At this point, I don't even care anymore. I used to enter situations caring about whether people liked me or wanted to be my friend. But now, I've reached a point in my life where I simply don't care. Well, I care, but in a different way. You know what I'm saying? I know who I am. I know that anything I put effort into, my intentions are always good. At the end of the day, I need to stay true to myself.

This way, others can't manipulate and make me feel guilty about a situation. This book has had a significant impact, I can't even fully express it. Whenever I read it, it's like a reminder that I'm now doing the things you used to do.

Life and career are about more than just being liked or seeking approval. It's about staying true to myself, as the saying goes: "I'm not going to set myself on fire in order to keep you warm." Yes, I'll be authentic and live my truth. And if you don't want to walk beside me, that's okay.

I think you should listen because I have the right answer. You should love me because I am the most genuine and caring person you will ever meet. But if you want to do it your own way or find another path besides what I'm offering, go ahead. I care, but I don't. I care about your destiny and your process, but I don't care needing you to acknowledge me. I'm not going to sacrifice myself or put myself in second place just to please you. This isn't about coddling you. You're not my child, and it's often not a life-or-death situation. You're simply being stubborn. I'm not going to be a pushover. I won't do something just to make you feel okay. As a leader, I don't have time for all that.

There was a time in my life when I didn't know how to handle situations like this. I wasn't confrontational, and I struggled to stand up for myself. But this experience is pushing me to stretch and tap into inner strengths I've always struggled with. Regardless of whether I hate or love this world, it's teaching me so much about myself. It's like a reminder that, "Hey, you have what it takes to handle it."

And now that I'm doing it, I approach it with a newfound confidence. I remind myself that, at the end of the day, I know who I am. So if you want to feel a certain way about me or the situation, that's fine. But from my perspective, it's not like that. It's either you're on board or you're not. There's no in-between. Yeah, and I don't care if you don't like me. I really don't. I mean it when I say it. But it's different now, you know? Yeah, that's what it is. I'm not responsible for whether you like me or not. **That's, that's your choice. I can't make your choice for you. I know I'm great.**

Having this job has helped me clarify what I want to do with my career. Initially, it was eldercare and group homes, but now I am open to pursuing therapy and establishing my own private practice. Surprisingly, as I do therapy on the side, I'm realizing how much I enjoy it, even though I never thought I could actually do it before. I used to wonder how I could possibly provide therapy to someone I didn't know much about. I had doubts and overthought it, but the more I engage in it, the more I understand, just like you mentioned in our previous conversation when I started working in group homes. I don't really want to do that anymore.

I'm grateful for the experience though, because it has taught me a lot and provided me with valuable learning opportunities. I now know that therapy is something I truly want to pursue. I want to continue writing my books and also thrive in my therapy practice. Ultimately, I want to obtain my license and fully commit to this path.

I began to realize the impact I was making when clients started expressing their motivation to schedule future appointments or inquiring about outside services after their program ended. They would ask if I provided therapy outside of our sessions because they wanted to continue working with me. This was a significant moment for me because it validated that I was truly making a difference in their lives.

Initially, I had doubts about myself, but hearing this reassurance from my clients was a powerful affirmation. It made me realize that I understood them on a deep level. As I took the time to learn about different therapeutic modalities, I initially had a superficial understanding of concepts like CBT and motivation. However, as I delved deeper and developed my own relationship with these modalities, I gained a solid comprehension of their application.

Understanding these modalities helped me make therapy more conversational and comfortable for my clients. I began to have a holistic approach and viewed clients not just through the lens of their circumstances but as complex individuals. I acknowledged the interconnectedness of their mental and emotional well-being with everything happening in their lives. This realization allowed me to provide more effective and comprehensive support to my clients.

## Chapter 7: ACHIEVEMENT - The Legacy From my Parents

I explore a personal journey of self-reflection and contemplation. It is here that I begin to understand the influence of my family and upbringing on shaping who I am today, while also acknowledging that my aspirations have led me in a different direction.

I realize that my parents were still teenagers when my older sister was born. They never completed high school, and their lives took a turn for the worse. My mother became entangled in the world of drugs, while my father found solace in the arms of another woman. Consequently, they lacked the resources and motivation needed to pursue a better life. Unfortunately, the negative impact of their choices also affected my siblings and me.

There were times when I couldn't help but envy those who seemed to have an easier life, wondering what my circumstances would have been like if my parents had left me with something to fall back on. I vividly recall the tears that welled up in my eyes as I questioned why my life had to be so hard. I even found myself resenting my grandmother for not being able to provide me with something as simple as a cell phone when my classmates were receiving cars as graduation gifts.

However, as I matured, I began to realize that material possessions did not necessarily equate to a better life. I came to understand that it's not about what I was given, but rather how I used my own inner strength and determination to create a better future for myself. I stopped blaming my parents for the challenges I faced and started taking responsibility for my own actions.

Throughout my journey of grief, I discovered the power of solitude. Although being alone can be daunting, it does offer an opportunity for self-reflection and personal growth. It is in these moments of solitude that I gained a clearer perspective on life and found the strength to forge my own path.

While my family and upbringing may have influenced me in certain ways, I have come to realize that I have the power to chart my own course. I am not defined by the circumstances in which I was raised or the choices my parents made. Instead, I have learned to embrace my own aspirations and work tirelessly to achieve them.

Moving forward, I understand that my journey will not be easy. The support I have comes solely from my grandmother, who has always been there for me, even though she does not have much to spare. It is in her love and encouragement that I find solace and strength.

**Hardships and Making the Life My Parents Could Not Provide**

So now I find myself in this section of the book, reflecting on all that has happened to me. Despite landing on my feet, there's still this nagging feeling about my parents.

I think what I recently experienced, especially in the context of getting married, connects to what I'm discussing now. But let's go back to when I was in school, contemplating whether it was the right path for me. However, deep down, I don't believe that was ever the real issue. I was always convinced, even when considering the influence of my parents, that I needed to pursue something greater. Ultimately, it wasn't about proving anything, as we previously talked about.

As I reflect on my relationship with my parents, I am torn between feelings of resentment and love. I cannot deny the impact of their actions on my life, but I have chosen not to let that define my journey. Instead, I have learned to work hard and fiercely pursue what I want in life.

Let's delve into how this relates to the pieces of my relationship with my parents. One aspect that stands out is the tug-of-war between feelings of resentment and love when it comes to them. What's intriguing is how I've channeled that conflict into working hard and striving for success. The phrase that resonates with me is creating a life that my parents couldn't provide for me. To me, it represents the drive I've developed amidst grief.

Even though I miss my parents and grapple with conflicting emotions of resentment and love, I have to come to terms with the reality and find ways to cope with it. Dealing with this situation has been a long journey, but I've reached a point of acceptance. In a way, it is what it is, and I have to do what I need to do to become the person I aspire to be.

I've learned to accept the grief process and find peace within it. I used to cry and question why my life had to be so challenging, why I had to work so hard for everything I wanted. I vividly recall a time when I reached out to someone for support, feeling overwhelmed when my car broke down, wondering aloud why everything had to be so difficult. However, I've now shifted my mindset to one of acceptance.

I understand that this is the hand I've been dealt, and I can't change it. It has become somewhat easier to navigate through adversities and setbacks because I've embraced the reality and the need to work through them. I used to ask why my life had to be so hard, why everything required so much effort, even ordinary things like getting my first cell phone or car.

So, it's all about acceptance for me. I finally reached a point where I accepted my situation, and my perspective shifted. I realized that I just have to do what I have to do. If I want something, I have to accept that it is what it is and work for it without dwelling on the difficulties. I stopped crying about why my life is so hard and accepted that this is the way it is now.

I like what Dr. Wright said about focusing on what I want to be rather than what I don't have or how hard it is. My motivation now is centered around who I want to become, and I know that I must put in the work to get there.

**The Family You Create**
Listening to motivational speakers like TD Jakes has also been helpful. He made a point that really resonated with me - it's not about what God took away, but rather, making the best of what I still have. He assured me that even with what is left of me, I can still thrive and become the person I desire to be. So, despite the challenges, I've been fortunate to be surrounded by great people who have helped shape me into who I am today.

It took years for my perspective to shift, but I no longer look at things in the same way. Like I mentioned before, my drive went from questioning and feeling defeated to simply accepting that it is what it is.

I believe that there's no set timeline for achieving your goals, if you continue to believe in yourself. It took me years to graduate from school, and people would often ask me when I would finish. But deep down, I knew that the timeframe didn't matter if I never gave up. I was determined and had a strong desire to accomplish it.

If you truly want something, trust the process even when it feels difficult or impossible. Surrounding yourself with the right people also plays a big role. Sometimes, you need to disconnect from family, social media, certain people, or situations that may hinder your progress. This allows you to focus on what you truly want.

It's important to realize that not everyone will understand your vision for yourself. Instead of telling everyone about your goals, it's better to reach a point where you understand that not everyone will comprehend what you see for yourself. Many people didn't understand my journey, so I stopped sharing it. And then, when I achieved my goals, they were surprised and didn't even know I was in school. It's essential to be okay with the fact that others may not see your vision or prioritize your personal goals.

After a while, graduating became a personal goal for myself. The number of years didn't matter anymore. I just knew deep down that I would get it done. I had to enjoy the journey and the present moment, as you advised me. I had to be optimistic and believe that everything I went through was necessary for me to reach this point. I saw the time it took as a necessary part of my journey, and I embraced it as a valuable learning experience.

When I eventually reach each destination along the journey, I know I will be fully prepared and equipped because I went through every step and setback along the way. Sometimes, it's necessary to go through challenges and setbacks to learn and grow. I gained a lot of wisdom and lessons from those difficult moments.

I may not have all the answers, but I have learned the importance of patience and perseverance in achieving my goals.

**After a while I stopped sharing my goals. People would remind me that I hadn't arrived. I began to share my accomplishments instead. Now they're speechless seeing how I've grown. – Georgia L. James**

### Finding A Greater Reason to Continue

Proving them wrong was a motivation. Whether it was family, other students, professors, or colleagues in the workplace, I had something to prove originally. That motivation has given way to a higher purpose. I have been able to make a significant impact on the lives of others and help them process their experiences. In the process, I have also learned a lot about myself. As I started receiving positive feedback, it not only felt good for me, but it also shifted my perspective on therapy. Initially, I approached it with a sense of obligation, like "Oh God, I have to do this therapy." However, as I continued working with clients in group homes, it became a calling for me. I genuinely enjoyed listening to people and being present for those meaningful moments.

This realization came after I noticed the impact I was having on others and everything started to make sense. It was like a transition from having theoretical knowledge from books and figuring out how to apply it practically. I went from having all this information to understanding how to make it relevant, not just for my clients, but for myself as well. I learned how to establish a therapeutic alliance and make it an authentic and meaningful experience.

Initially, I didn't even understand what people meant when they said I was authentic. But through interacting with many individuals who were inauthentic or putting on facades, it became clear to me. I realized that I naturally embodied authenticity without even trying. I used to struggle with this aspect of myself because I thought it made me appear weak. However, as you mentioned before, people actually aspire to be like someone with my genuine characteristics. I began to appreciate and embrace myself more, understanding that there are people in the world who genuinely need someone like me, especially those who are struggling with depression or other challenges.

This journey has allowed me to cultivate a deep sense of empathy and a desire to help others. I used to wonder how I could make a difference, but now I see that the key is simply listening. By truly hearing and understanding others, I can provide the support they need.

## Chapter 8: CONFIDENCE - Confirming My Purpose

At that I decided to enter the MSW education, I was working at a call center, doing what I would call telehealth social work. I quickly realized that in that setting, the atmosphere was always quiet and you weren't allowed to talk or get up and interact with people. This was a constant source of trouble for me. I found myself at risk of losing my job because I couldn't be myself. I always had a natural inclination to walk around and help people, it was just who I was. That's when a lady suggested that I should consider going back to my social work roots, because I shouldn't let these restrictions take away my true passion.

I missed the work itself and I always had a desire to work in a hospital setting. So, I started applying for jobs in hospitals. However, I quickly realized that most of these positions required a master's degree. This was a major obstacle for me, as I had never wanted to do case management work and I didn't want to settle for anything less than working in a hospital. This realization prompted me to go back and get my master's degree.

Going back to school and juggling the demands of a full-blown family was incredibly challenging. At that time, my kids were involved in various activities and were no longer babies. I was working full-time and even had two jobs. To add to it all, I had to find time for school work. It was a lot to manage and I often found myself feeling overwhelmed.

Compared to my undergraduate experience, there were a lot of different moving pieces in my life during my master's program. The key difference was that my kids were older and more self-sufficient. If I had to do class work after coming home from work, they would take care of themselves by going to the kitchen and cooking their own meals.

During my undergraduate years, when Harmony was a baby, I had to take her with me everywhere I went. Whether it was to class or work, she would be by my side. Finding someone to watch her for me was a constant challenge. However, during my master's program, my job was more flexible as I was able to work from home. The majority of my internship was also conducted remotely due to the COVID pandemic. I didn't have to commute anywhere, which made things a little easier. Although COVID made things virtual, it also added a heavier workload to my plate.

**Applying My Grief Knowledge**

If I haven't mentioned it before, my husband Jerall has two children prior to our daughter Harmony: Tip, the oldest, and Serenity just behind him in age. From early on in our relationship, Jerall made it clear that he co-parents with their mother. We would often have the kids for extended weekends and holidays, but I was never particularly close or distant with their mother. We interacted cordially on a need-to basis.

As I approached the end of my MSW program, I received a distressing call from the kids' mother. She knew that I was a social worker, and what I had accomplished. It was the year that she passed away and we all caught COVID. Those two hardships made things even more difficult for us. It was like things kicked up a notch because of her passing.

She passed away due to complications from diabetes, which was quite unexpected. We had talked to her on FaceTime, and she didn't let on the severity of her illness. We didn't know what she was trying to tell us when she asked for my help in telling her kids that she loved them. It was only later that day that we got a phone call, where we were told that she had an infection that had spread throughout her body, and they were going to have to amputate her limbs. Despite this, she didn't want to live like that and chose to pass away. This revelation was a shock for all of us, and it was then that things got very difficult. Tip and Serenity were quite young at the time, and they didn't understand the situation entirely. After her passing, I knew that I had to step up and take more responsibility.

I was initially hurt because I felt like Jerall never put the burden of being a mother to his children on me. I had always treated them as my own, but their mother was supposed to be here, not me. I had to reassure Jerall that even though their mother was gone, I was still here for him and the kids.

I had to continue showing Serenity maternal love and support, understanding that she needed that presence in her life. My grandmother played a crucial role in helping me navigate this situation. She reminded me that I was the best person for Serenity right now because I had also experienced losing my own mother at a young age.

**Retraumatization or Recovery**

It felt like I was reliving my own life all over again, and that realization hit me hard. I wondered if this was a repetition of my past, if history would repeat itself with the father figure also leaving us.

My mind immediately went to that place of fear and uncertainty. I thought, "Oh my God, is this a repeat of my own life? Serenity is the same age as me when my mother died, and now Jerall could also die." I had to gather myself because I wasn't in a good state of mind. Once I composed myself, I was able to be there for them because they were all struggling.

It was tough. It felt like a retraumatization of past events. However, it made sense considering that when I submitted my last assignment for my doctorate, I couldn't help but cry tears of relief and accomplishment. I felt like I had made it through the challenges. The important lesson I learned was that throughout it all, the kids and Jerall stood by my side. It hurt me to think, "When will I have someone there for me?", realizing that my parents aren't around, unlike these two who have been there consistently.

I had my moments of doubt and worry, but the crucial realization was that they have always supported me. They have stood by me through thick and thin. Jerall has made sacrifices for me to pursue my education, and I'm grateful for that. Even the kids have shown up and been present during times when I was juggling so many responsibilities, like work, assignments, and internships. They were mature and understanding.

It's important for people to realize that others will show up for them when it matters. We should expect and demand that people show up for us when we need them, but at the same time, we should also be there for them. The ones who truly matter will be there for us when we need them. I learned that in this process, despite everything, Jerall and his kids are always there. He always finds a way to make me happy and does things for me. He truly cares and supports me.

## Chapter 9: EXCELLENCE - New Lessons Rising Above

Graduation marked the beginning of a new chapter as I entered the workforce. However, I found myself frequently questioning my mentor about how I could gain the confidence to stand before bosses and coworkers. I started working in a group home, and while I don't want to delve into all the problems that arose, I'd rather focus on the valuable lessons I learned. Let's just say it was a classic case of being overworked, underpaid, and lacking the necessary resources, with an expectation that I wouldn't voice any complaints.

I was constantly second-guessed, made to feel inadequate, and kept isolated. I pushed myself to work over 60 hours per week, neglecting my home life and my own well-being. I even brought work home after long, exhausting 10-hour days. Looking back now, I realize that wasn't a healthy approach.

Eventually, I made the decision to quit my job. Not long after, my assistant also resigned. Later that week, I received word from a former employee that the company was shutting down operations in the area. It turned out that I was the one holding everything together, which was oddly satisfying but also infuriating. The pressure I felt was real, yet they refused to acknowledge it or provide the support I needed. There was no interest in improving my pay or addressing my complaints, but I was carrying the weight of the entire company on my shoulders.

Unfortunately, my health started deteriorating as a result. My confidence was constantly being challenged, and I began to fear potential health issues like blood clots and heart problems. I had abandoned my exercise routine, neglected my family engagements, and lost touch with so many aspects that define who I am. Now that I've quit, I can see just how much of myself I had lost in that toxic environment.

I am currently prioritizing a return to myself and focusing on self-care as a way to improve my mental health. You mentioned a while ago that this book is exactly what I need to invest my energy into, so I feel like it's a form of self-care for me.

It's important for me to be consistent with self-care and to continue beyond just reading this book. I know that there will be other things that come to mind as well.

**Managing the Complexity**

My reflections on self-care are not just about general self-care but also about how getting married and finishing school have presented new opportunities for me. While the pain of loss is still there, I'm working on transforming it into inspiration and motivation for my life. This is one way to understand self-care. I believe that my new outlook on life influences both my future and my past pain.

Well, I feel like this particular field has always been a passion for me. However, with my previous job, I started experiencing fatigue and burnout. I noticed that my passion and empathy for people were fading away, and I knew that a big part of it was because I had neglected my own self-care needs. I didn't pay attention to my emotions and didn't give myself the necessary time and attention. Instead of recognizing when I needed to take a break or step away, I pushed myself to keep going. I stopped getting my hair done and neglected regular monthly massages, not because of financial reasons, but simply because I never made time for them. Other things always took priority over self-care, and I never took the time to pause and prioritize myself.

I kept pushing myself, relentlessly trying to complete job responsibilities and tasks, even when I felt completely burnt out. It didn't matter if the tasks were simple or complex, I just felt drained and exhausted all the time. Even in my side job, a field I had always been passionate about, I started losing interest. I couldn't understand where these feelings were coming from.

Why was I feeling this way about helping and talking to people, something I had always wanted to do? I just couldn't find the motivation anymore. I found myself wanting to stay in bed and not work anymore. There was a time when I used to enjoy getting up and doing this type of job, even when the pay wasn't sufficient. It was a sense of fulfillment that kept me going. But now, I just didn't feel it anymore.

As time went on, I started noticing physical symptoms. My body was constantly hurting, my feet and knees were in pain. I realized that I wasn't eating right, and I started experiencing heartburn, something I hadn't had in years. It became clear that stress was leading me to make unhealthy eating choices, and pizza seemed to be the only comfort I sought. My chest and heart were also hurting, adding to my concerns. I knew deep down that this was a result of neglecting my self-care.

My body was signaling that something was wrong, and at 34, I knew it was because I was overwhelmed and unhappy. It wasn't just about my personal life; it was about ignoring my emotions and neglecting my mental and emotional well-being.

Everything happened for a reason and at the right time. There was a specific moment when I woke up one morning and just realized that I was done. It wasn't a contemplation process leading up to that moment; it was a sudden feeling of exhaustion. This particular situation was the utmost disrespect, and I questioned who they thought they were talking to.

At that point, I decided that I didn't want to fight anymore. It wasn't worth it. I knew I was doing my best, but I felt like I was constantly trying to prove myself to everyone. It seemed like everyone was attacking me, and I didn't have the energy to keep fighting for their approval. That was my breaking point. And then, on top of that, my assistant quit.

A week later, I received an email from another employee who still worked there, informing me that the company was shutting down. Since that day, I have felt an incredible sense of peace. It's a relief to know that my phone isn't constantly ringing, that I'm not overwhelmed with questions and emails. I'm no longer getting questioned about why I haven't replied or bothered by staff calling me about every little thing. They have no idea where my mind has been.

I'm sure you understand where my mind is at right now - at rest. This feeling is something I haven't experienced in a long time, and it made me realize that I need to prioritize self-care. Even though I'm undergoing therapy, I've been neglecting my own needs. Taking care of myself is not a luxury; it's a necessity, and I need to do better.

So this morning, I decided to establish a morning ritual and routine. Since my therapy job at home requires me to work from 4 to 1, I figured I might as well start my day early. I woke up at 4 o'clock and started by brushing my teeth. Then, I engaged in a meditation session and listened to motivational speeches by TD Jakes. I also followed a strength training exercise on YouTube.

Today was my first day, and I managed to spend 10 minutes on my Stairmaster. I even pushed myself to do another 10 minutes. Additionally, I did 40 squats. My goal is to establish a consistent routine where I engage in these activities regularly. Starting my day off feeling good is important to me. It sets the tone for the rest of the day.

**The Grief Coda**

I started thinking about death recently, and it gives me anxiety. Whenever it crosses my mind, I have to tell myself that everything is okay. This hasn't happened in a long time, but it's been showing up periodically. I don't like thinking about it because it triggers severe anxiety.

I guess it started when I started focusing on my self-care. My body started hurting a bit, and that made me feel uneasy, though I'm not entirely sure why. My chest was hurting and it made me think about my own mortality. I talked about this before with my mentor when discussing leaving my job and prioritizing myself, specifically giving myself time instead of giving it all to my job. I'm starting to realize that taking care of myself and Harmony are more important than any career aspirations.

It is anxiety or insight; however I choose to look at it. My revelation is a reflection on what my parents couldn't do. I am dealing with something now that my parents did not face, faced and failed, or never had the chance to face. I am choosing me AND choosing others. I am deciding to be my healthiest so that I can give Harmony, the other kids, and my husband a foundation of peace and joy upon which to build their best life.

They weren't able to look at themselves and make the decision to change their situation and be better for themselves and their children. It's fascinating that you're facing that right now and saying, "No, I can change this situation. I can be better." The fear may arise because the stakes are high, but it doesn't have to be fear. It can be motivation because you have the power to make choices and take action. It's not about having a advanced degrees, but about being a person with a brain who can make better choices.

You can choose to be disciplined and consistent, and through these choices, you will bring about positive changes. You've already outlined the great things that will come from making these changes.

As you reflect on your parents and the choices they didn't make, I want to emphasize that they were also humans with brains. They could have made better choices, sought new information, asked for help, or read books. Holding them accountable is the same as holding yourself accountable. You love them, grieve for them, but you can still acknowledge their shortcomings. Holding them accountable is important because it means holding yourself accountable too.

I agree with you. This moment is yours to make the decision and take action. Now, when you think about that answer, what parts are most personal to you in relation to your own choices and their choices?

When I reflect on my past and my upbringing, I remember the emotions I experienced after my parents passed away. I wouldn't wish that on anybody, and especially not on Harmony. I can't even believe I went through it myself. It's something I would never want my own child to go through. So, it's personal to me in that aspect. I remember the emotions, thoughts, and everything that came with the death of my parents. It was a lot to handle, and I wouldn't want Harmony to experience it and try to navigate through it.

**Job Market Moving Forward**

It's important to feel good and regain that sense of freedom. It reminds me of when I used to do this in school - getting up early, going to the gym. It became a routine that made me feel good, and I want to get back to that. I want to feel stress-free.

I have one job now, and I'm not going to overthink or feel any kind of way about it. I'm starting to inform my confidence with a work ethic that is smarter and holistic. I have my master's degree, and if a job can't give me what I want, I'm turning it down. I've already turned down two jobs because I'm focused on myself and tired of wasting money.

Working two jobs, constantly running and processing new information, is mentally draining. I'm tired of chasing after money. I'm turning down jobs that don't accommodate my schedule. I'm really committing to taking care of myself. Part of that is recognizing that I have my master's degree and that I'm already doing counseling and therapy work. I'm doing the tasks that should be assigned to a licensed professional, and if they don't want to pay me for those skills, I'll stay where I am until I get my licensure or find a place that values me and pays appropriately.

I'm okay with a salary range of $68,000 to $70,000. I'm not being bougie about it, but I'm tired of chasing money. I've always worked multiple jobs, crazy hours, and I've been exhausted. I've neglected my husband and kids and haven't been the fun parent that I used to be. The demands of the jobs left me with nothing to give them except the bare minimum. It's frustrating because the things they want to do are things I used to do with them. But due to the imbalance caused by chasing jobs, I don't have the energy or time for it.

Now that I'm getting older, I realize the importance of prioritizing self-care and finding that balance.

# Section III: Healing My Inner Child

## Chapter 10: Self-Discovery with Family Dynamic

My family has always been a source of complexity for me. When I made the decision to get married, it brought up all the emotions of growing up and the loss I experienced. It was overwhelming, but I knew I needed to process these feelings and learn more about myself in the process.

With my cousins, I've always felt like I'm on the outside looking in. There's this pressure to conform, and I often find myself walking on eggshells around them. But I've come to realize that I move differently. They can sense that I'm comfortable being different, and that sets me apart from them. I used to desperately try to fit into their circle, but now I embrace my authenticity.

However, I've noticed that when it comes to authenticity, there seems to be a lack of empathy and compassion, particularly when it comes to disrespect. Certain comments and situations trigger past traumas, but I struggle to respond because my degree and education are often used against me. It's frustrating that they can lean on me for free therapy, but can't acknowledge that my education is what enables me to relate to them.

I think at the moment, I haven't made up my mind about it. Before, it was there, but now it's hitting differently. Maybe it's because I'm getting older, or maybe because I'm making different connections and looking at things differently. I previously had my mind made up, but now I'm not sure.

When it comes to my family dynamic, I feel like my siblings could understand, but my grandma, aunties, and cousins might struggle. I'm not as close to them as I used to be, and I'm not sure if they would take it seriously or understand how I'm feeling.

I feel like I see things differently, and I'm more introspective than most people realize, especially my family. They might only see the surface, but I am very deep and look at things in ways that they might not understand or take seriously.

If I had to write a letter to them, I would talk about making different choices, but I'm not sure if they would fully comprehend it. It feels like the things that are important to me and the way I see things are much deeper than what they might be aware of.

**Getting Deeper**

There are deep thoughts and perspectives that I have that they may not fully comprehend. For example, there's this whole "bougie" thing that my family likes to say, implying that I'm bougie because I pay my car note on time. But I believe that responsibility and financial stability are not bougie, they are just basic adulting. These are just some examples of the disconnect in our thinking.

Another aspect is their emphasis on family. While they value getting together and being a close-knit unit, they also have a tendency to put others down or make you feel like you can't truly be yourself. It's like we have to adhere to a certain way of being around them. But I have reached a point where I can't just go along with it because that's not who I am. I can't pretend to be okay with it when I'm not.

What bothers me is the lack of empathy and compassion they seem to have, and the way they minimize or brush off the impact certain things can have on someone. When they talk about sensitive topics or fail to show respect, it triggers me. I have to laugh it off and pretend like everything is okay, but deep down, my heart is racing and I feel uncomfortable. It's like they don't see the problem with it, and if I were to express my feelings, they would just dismiss me as the social worker in the family, not taking it seriously. But it goes so much deeper than that, and I wish they could understand.

Because of these dynamics, I find myself feeling disconnected from my own family. I often feel closer to my friends and have a stronger relationship with them than with my own relatives. When I say family, I think I need to be more specific, because my experience with them is quite different.

I strongly believe in the power of embracing the bougie lifestyle and not being ashamed of it. I would tell anyone who is willing to listen that being bougie is the way to go. It's about breaking free, forging your own path, and taking ownership of your life. Sure, there may be obstacles along the way, but the essence of being bougie is not backing down. Those who discourage it are simply basic individuals without depth. Every bougie person can confidently back up their choices and lifestyle. So, my message is clear: don't resist being bougie. It's time to embrace it wholeheartedly and unapologetically.

When I talk about my cousins, especially the ones I grew up with in the same household, I realize that their focus is always on themselves and their immediate siblings. It's like I'm now an outsider looking in, seeing them for who they truly are. But I have to maintain this facade or they can sense that I no longer care about being part of their circle.

You see, when I say cousins, I'm referring specifically to my actual first cousins. We all grew up as brothers because our grandma raised us. But they are all siblings and I'm the cousin. I've distanced myself from all of that now, and I honestly don't care anymore.

There was a time when I was desperate to be part of their circle, begging for their acceptance. But as I find my own identity, I realize that it hurts the most because they aren't really there for me. They are just there for each other. And I'm not okay with that. However, there is one sibling who calls me and talks to me about certain things because, deep down, they know they can't discuss those issues with their own sisters or brothers. That's why they reach out to me. It's a unique connection, and we keep those conversations between us because we understand each other in a way that others can't.

**Deeper Meaning of Autonomy**

In black families, it's often a big deal when someone achieves education or status that leads them to move out of the neighborhood. Suddenly, we become different, like outsiders looking in. And then, they try to belittle us or use our success as a reason to exclude us from their circle. It's frustrating, and your discussion is triggering some of those emotions within me.

However, I'd prefer if we focused on something more productive. I've heard comments like, "Here we go with the big words. The social worker is speaking!" said sarcastically. But I won't talk to you as if you're a third grader. I won't break things down and explain everything because then you might accuse me of patronizing you. No matter what I do, I can't seem to win their approval. It feels like I have to walk on eggshells, trying to fit in with them when deep down, I know I'm not the same person anymore. I'm not "Gege on the block" anymore; now, I'm "Gege the professional," and they'll just have to deal with it.

I've come to realize that I used to beg them to be part of their circle, but now I understand the importance of being different. And when they finally grasp that, they'll come to me when they need someone with a professional perspective, seeking what feels like free therapy. And I don't mind helping them progress when they genuinely want to.

I have become very comfortable with being the person I am. I can offer you help, but it depends on whether you're interested in hearing what I have to say. That's important to keep in mind.

I think what you're trying to express is that sometimes it feels like the person you're talking to is ashamed of showing their true self. It's like they put on a front or hide certain aspects of who they are. And it's not that you don't know that side of them, but it feels like they don't want others to see it, or they're ashamed of it. It's challenging to find the right words to describe this feeling, but you're doing a good job explaining it.

It's true that people who are inauthentic or try to hide their true selves often experience anxiety. And as a result, they may turn to self-medication, such as alcohol or promiscuity, to cope with their anxiety and depression. It leads to chaos in their lives, with multiple complicated relationships. If they could just be genuine and embrace who they truly are, they would find a sense of peace. That's something I am keen on demonstrating by being true to myself.

**Setting the Example Rather than Fighting for Change**

The best way to educate people is by setting an example through your own success. I've realized that this is the only way to handle certain situations. When others see you thriving, it opens their eyes to the possibilities and opportunities available to them.

My cousin recently expressed to me that she looks up to me because she's planning to move to Texas. Currently, she lives in Ohio with my grandma, and my grandma often associates the two of us together. She believes that both Ariana and I are resilient and can overcome any challenges. My cousin called me and said, "If you can do it, then I can do it too." She sees everything I've accomplished, and it's inspired her to take action. She's now planning to move to Texas, even though she doesn't have any family or support there. She has a husband in the military and a baby who is only three or four years old.

Her desire to follow in my footsteps is evident. She originally wanted to pursue social work, and now she's making this big move. I remember when I moved to Nashville to pursue my master's degree, she called me. Her brother had just obtained his bachelor's degree, and she said to me, "If I look up to anyone, it's you because you achieved all of this with a baby." Although she hasn't openly expressed this admiration in front of her siblings, she's been talking about it with them, and they're actually supporting her decision to move to Texas.

This will be her first major move, and she's only 22 years old. Our grandma sees both Ariana and me as the ones who can handle challenging situations and find solutions. She knows that Ariana has been a great help to her, and she'll surely miss her. However, our grandma always mentions me and how I can make things happen no matter what. Ariana is excited about this new chapter in her life, but she can't believe she's actually doing it. She has never explicitly told anyone that she looks up to me, but I can tell by the way she talks.

But you know, most importantly, my daughter Harmony is the one who truly looks up to me. That's what matters the most to me.

# Chapter 11: Journey of Healing and Self-Realization

Believing in yourself is crucial, because if you don't have that self-belief, it's unlikely that others will have it in you either. When you start to believe in yourself, something amazing happens – you walk and talk with a newfound confidence and your overall demeanor begins to flourish. I experienced this firsthand during our conversation today. I felt so articulate and fluent in expressing my emotions because I reminded myself of who I truly am.

**The Confidence Came from the Testimonials**
In the past, I would pursue any job that came my way without hesitation. But recently, I turned down two job offers. It's a significant shift for me. I now realize that I have the power to choose the opportunities that align with my goals and aspirations. I have the confidence that I will pass my upcoming test because I've started to comprehend and internalize the information in a whole new way. It used to be a struggle for me to make sense of the material, but now, as I read it, things are clicking into place and making sense. I no longer have to read it multiple times to grasp the concepts. Something has shifted within me, and it's all because I am wholeheartedly believing in myself and my abilities.

During my morning routine, I immerse myself in motivational speeches. It sets the tone for my day and provides a strong foundation.

One particular speech mentioned the importance of nurturing a child's skills and talents. It got me thinking and prompted deep self-reflection.

I began to question if I had been cultivating my own skills and talents, truly believing in them and unlocking my full potential. It made me realize the significance of investing in myself, just as we would support and encourage a child to pursue their passions. I've recognized that I have unique abilities and capabilities that deserve recognition and development.

Believing in oneself is not an overnight process. It takes time, effort, and self-reflection. But once we truly embrace and trust in ourselves, the possibilities become endless.

As I continue on this journey of self-belief, I am aware of the positive changes it is bringing to my life. Not only am I becoming more confident, but I am also discovering new aspects of my identity and abilities. Each day, I am reminded that I have the power to create my own destiny and pursue my dreams.

Believing in myself has allowed me to reject the notion of settling for less than what I deserve. It has empowered me to take control of my choices and strive for the future I envision. With each step forward, I know that I am capable of achieving greatness. The hurdles that may come my way are mere opportunities for growth and learning.

So, I will continue to nurture my self-belief and encourage it to flourish. I will celebrate every milestone along the way and remain committed to believing in myself even in the face of doubts or setbacks. Because, ultimately, the belief I have in myself is the driving force behind my success, fulfillment, and happiness.

**Making Sense, Decision Making, and Clarifying Directions**

During my younger years, I would frequently visit a nursing home near my house. Despite my Grandma's suspicions about my intentions, it was actually my way of cultivating my own passion.

Unbeknownst to me at the time, I was already honing my interpersonal skills by working and interacting with the elderly. I didn't fully grasp the significance of this experience until now. I have come to believe in myself and my abilities in a whole new way. This is what I am meant to do. I just need to refine and articulate it better.

Before, I would often stumble and feel intimidated when trying to express myself. I lacked confidence because I didn't fully understand certain concepts or topics. I would question myself and hesitate to voice my opinion out of fear of being wrong. But now, things have changed. I have gained a deeper understanding of my area of expertise. I no longer stutter or feel scared when engaging in conversations. I have the assurance that I know what I'm talking about. I have confidence in my abilities, most notably in this particular field where I excel.

What's even better is that I am finally being compensated for my work. In the past, I used to beg and pester people, pleading for an opportunity to assist them with their social work. But now, my perspective has shifted. I no longer feel the need to actively seek out individuals to lend a helping hand. I can confidently navigate deep discussions and provide support effortlessly. This is what I do, day in and day out. And now, I am being recognized and paid for it.

As I continue to embrace and explore my passion, I am particularly drawn to the challenges and opportunities presented in working with this specific population.

I am continuously working on my professional development, even with my documentation. I am striving to learn how to incorporate intervention verbs and proper terminology to make my work sound better. The scripts provided to us are not enough for me, as I am taking therapy materials that break down each modality and how to incorporate them with precise language. This includes the proper use of intervention terminology and documentation.

I searched for a resource called "Comment Intervention Terminology and Documentation" to learn and become more proficient in making my work sound good. I want to be that person who can articulate their thoughts and ideas clearly. It may seem trivial, but it matters to me, and it translates to better care for my clients.

For me, the significance of gathering information and reinforcing my confidence cannot be overstated. It is essential to seek out knowledge, especially in the area of expertise, to be better at what I am passionate about. It is crucial to inform oneself for the benefit of others.

Sometimes, people who do not understand my choices may cast judgment, but I am doing what is best for myself and for the people I care about. Making different choices is not always easy, but it is worth it. That's why I keep informing myself and developing my skills so I can provide the best care possible.

**Good People**

I had to face the death of my loved ones, and amidst the grief, I discovered something unexpected. One might assume that overcoming such a loss would lead to improved health and healing. However, what truly emerged from that experience was the belief in oneself and the recognition of a deeper spirituality. Although my parents are no longer here, I embrace the spirituality that I believe they would have wanted for me. Deep down, I knew their desires and took the opportunity to fill that void in my life. I found surrogate parents who offered their support, and I grasped that opportunity tightly.

Accepting help, engaging with positive individuals, making better choices for oneself, and letting go of dysfunction and toxicity are crucial life skills that many people need in today's world. It's disheartening that sometimes, when you show others the path to health and well-being, they dismiss it as something detrimental. In my heart, I genuinely want to be there for others as a friend, offering support, providing good advice, and making them feel special. It perplexes me that people often fail to recognize the value of such relationships.

Allow me to share a specific incident that illustrates this issue. I worked with a maintenance man at a previous job, who happened to be a fantastic individual. He was a black man, and although his background check did not come back clear, the company decided to keep him on as a contractor since he had already started working for us. I recall talking to him about a maintenance request and, in passing, he mentioned that his birthday was on a Saturday. I simply wanted to acknowledge him and show my respect, with no intention of flirting. To my surprise, his wife misinterpreted my well wishes as a sexual advance towards her husband. As a result, my supervisor instructed me to avoid any further contact with him.

This incident showcases the sad reality of today's society. Instead of recognizing the sincerity and goodwill behind my actions, people are quick to focus on the wrong things. This man, an older individual dedicated to his work, was unjustly targeted despite his lack of any inappropriate behavior. It was a disheartening situation that aligns with the points you mentioned earlier.

Cherish genuine connections, support one another, and be not swayed by misguided perceptions. Let us shift our focus to recognizing and appreciating acts of faith and sincerity when they are shown to us, rather than letting unnecessary concerns cloud our judgment.

**Speaking to Your Inner Child**

When we speak to our inner child, it's important to approach her with respect and admiration. Don't feel sorry for her. Respect her. She has endured countless challenges and has emerged victorious, creating a life for herself through the power of grace. Her determination and unwavering focus on her goals allowed her to achieve remarkable accomplishments.

Just think about her enrollment in Saginaw State, a decision made without any family members as examples to follow. Despite this, she recognized the support that was offered and took the leap by enrolling in classes. And let's not forget the bold move to Nashville, bravely undertaken without any family support. That was all her. She had the courage to chart her own path. Then there was the pivotal decision to transfer to TSU after a conversation with a counselor at MTSU. She listened to her intuition and made a choice aligned with her aspirations.

And let's not overlook the incredible achievement of obtaining a Master's degree. That girl grew up and fearlessly pursued her vision.

However, I now face a new challenge: redefining my perspective on loss. It's crucial to recognize that not all losses are actually losses. Losing contact with individuals who thrive on drama and bring negativity into my life is not a loss at all; it's a gain. It creates space for positive relationships and a healthier, more peaceful existence. Similarly, losing a job that places an excessive burden on my well-being and disregards my health is not a loss; it's an opportunity for growth and a chance to find a job that aligns with my values and supports my well-being.

I want to emphasize that I am not lacking or without because of these perceived losses. Instead, I choose to identify and be grateful for the blessings in my life. I am surrounded by wonderful people who provide me with unwavering support, and that is something to be cherished. It is through acknowledging these blessings and nurturing the relationship with my inner child that I can continue to grow, overcome challenges, and live a life filled with fulfillment and joy.

So, let us speak to our inner child with admiration and respect, honoring her journey and celebrating her accomplishments. Together, we can embrace the lessons learned from perceived losses and cultivate gratitude for the blessings that surround us, ensuring a path of continued growth and happiness.

# Appendix: Affirmations

## Affirmations For Healing Your Inner Child

Embarking on a transformative journey requires fortitude and a holistic approach—one that encompasses the various facets of our being. The GRACE acronym brings forth a foundation: Grief, Resilience, Achievement, Confidence, and Excellence. These are quintessential elements that foster healing and growth within ourselves. But to truly rise, one must also engage with the principles that lie Beyond GRACE: Faith, Persistence, Leverage, Learning, Courage, Adaptability, and Networking. These principles serve as powerful affirmations, guiding us toward untapped potential and a reinvigorated sense of self.

Consider, if you will, the power of Grief. It is not an abyss to escape but a teacher to embrace. The avenue of grief carves out the capacity for profound compassion both towards oneself and others, teaching us that in the heart of vulnerability lies our shared humanity. "I honor my grief as a testament to my capacity for love," could be an affirmation that empowers and legitimizes our emotional experiences, guiding us through the healing process.

Resilience arises from our unwavering spirit, an indomitable force that propels us through life's inevitable storms. It is the reservoir of strength that we tap into, enabling us to say, "I am the embodiment of resilience; every challenge is a catalyst for my growth."

Achievement, in this context, is not merely a marker of success but an ongoing journey marked by continuous learning and personal evolution. Achievement becomes an affirmation of progress: "I celebrate each step forward, for every milestone is a reflection of my commitment to my goals."

Confidence then is more than self-assurance—it is the intuitive knowledge that you are worthy, capable, and deserving of your dreams. It stands as a pillar for self-empowerment, whispering, "My confidence is unwavering because it is grounded in the truth of my abilities and worth."

Excellence is not perfection but the pursuit of one's highest potential. It is the sum of small efforts repeated day in and day out. With excellence, we affirm, "I strive for excellence in all I do, knowing that my best effort is the truest measure of my success."

Moving beyond GRACE, we meet affirmations rooted in deeper insight and higher aspirations. Faith, the bedrock of our journey, assures us that we are never alone—we are supported by a higher power and the universe, a force that aligns with our purpose. "I have faith that my path is unfolding exactly as it's meant to," we affirm, as we align ourselves with the greater good.

Persistence is the relentless pursuit of our vision, even in the face of obstacles. It is the determination that fuels our resilience. "I persist with perseverance, knowing that my passion will lead me to fulfill my purpose."

Leverage is the strategic utilization of resources, knowledge, and relationships. It's recognizing that we don't have to do it alone; we can amplify our impact by leveraging support. "I wisely leverage the strengths of my community to magnify my contributions."

Learning is the continuous endeavor to expand our minds and skillsets. It is lifelong and life-wide. "Through constant learning, I transform every experience into wisdom," we affirm.

Courage is the brave heart that leads us to step out of our comfort zone and into our power. "I embrace courage to act in spite of fear, knowing that my bravery shapes my destiny."

Adaptability is the fluidity that enables us to navigate change with grace and agility. "I am adaptable, easily adjusting to new situations and optimizing outcomes."

Networking is the cultivation of relationships that support and elevate. It's understanding that our connections can lead to synergies and mutual growth. "I build nurturing networks that serve collective advancement and personal enrichment."

These affirmations, rooted in the GRACE acronym and expanded by the Beyond GRACE Model, offer a theoretical framework to guide us through grief recovery, career development, work-life harmony, and ultimate self-care. Each one is a step, a breath, a leap into our most authentic selves. Consider them, embrace them, and let them guide you through the powerful odyssey of healing your inner child, transcending adversity, and sculpting a life of fulfillment. Together, let us walk this path, for in the harmonious blending of GRACE and Beyond GRACE, our potential is boundless.

# Grief

In the quiet chambers of the heart, where memories reside with the softest echo, let these affirmations be the light that guides you through the tapestry of grief. Each word is a thread, interwoven with the essence of Georgia's journey, reflecting the labyrinth of loss and the courage to step into its shadows.

1. "I give myself permission to feel the full spectrum of my emotions, recognizing that in my vulnerability lies my strength. Like Georgia, I understand that denying my grief is denying a part of my story, a part of me."
2. "With every tear that escapes, I cleanse a piece of my soul, allowing new growth in spaces once occupied by loss. Georgia's journey taught me that grief is not just an end but a genesis of deeper understanding."
3. "I am not alone in my sorrow; the universe cradles me in its understanding embrace. Just as Georgia found solace in the belief of something greater, I anchor my heart in the faith that I am supported."
4. "I embrace the memories, letting them flow freely—bittersweet reminders of love that transcends the physical realm. Georgia's reflection on cherishing each moment renews my gratitude for the gift of connection."
5. "I allow myself to move at my own pace, understanding that healing is not linear, but a journey with ebbs and flows. Inspired by Georgia's path, I honor my timeline, knowing each step forward is progress."
6. "In my darkest hours, I will remember that grief is a testament to the depth of my love. Georgia's experiences remind me that to grieve is to have loved profoundly."

7. "I cultivate resilience, knowing that with each challenge comes the opportunity for personal transformation. Observing Georgia's resilience empowers me to rise from the ashes of my despair."
8. "I hold space for my grief, allowing it to coexist with moments of joy, understanding that my heart has the capacity for both. Georgia's journey highlights the complex tapestry of human emotions."
9. "I reach out for support, embracing the strength found in vulnerability. Just as Georgia learned the value of community, I recognize I do not have to navigate my grief in solitude."
10. "I give myself grace, acknowledging that healing is not about finding closure but about learning to live with loss. Inspired by Georgia, I strive to weave my grief into the fabric of my life, a poignant reminder of love's everlasting impression."

Through these affirmations, let the essence of Georgia's memoir serve as a beacon, illuminating the path through the night of grief. Here, in the intimate dance of shadow and light, may you find solace and strength, embodying the courage to face each day with resilience and grace.

## Resilience

In the quiet, tender moments of reflection, where the heart sits softly amidst the ruins of what was and the promise of what is to come, let these affirmations on resilience gently wrap around your soul, whispering of strength, courage, and the unwavering light within, inspired by the journey shared in Georgia's memoir.

1. "Within me flows the courage of a thousand rivers, carving paths through the hardest stone of adversity. Like Georgia, I am the sculptor of my destiny, shaping my future with every resilient beat of my heart."
2. "I am a lighthouse, steadfast amidst the stormy seas of life's challenges. Drawing from Georgia's journey, I stand tall, my light unquenchable, guiding myself back to peace with unwavering resolve."
3. "Roots deep within the earth of my experiences anchor me in the face of life's gales. Georgia's resilience teaches me that though I may sway, I will not break, for my strength is as deep as it is silent."
4. "I breathe in resilience like a balm for the soul, exhaling the weight of despair. Each breath, a testament to my endurance, mirrors Georgia's journey through valleys shadowed by sorrow."
5. "In the tapestry of my life, resilience threads golden lines through dark patches, a pattern of triumph over trials. Witnessing Georgia's path, I am reminded that my story, too, will be woven with light amidst the darkness."
6. "I rise with the dawn, a symbol of hope and renewal. Just as Georgia faced each day with determination, I, too, embrace

the morning's light, finding within me an inexhaustible well of strength."
7. "My heart, a fortress built on the foundations of resilience, shelters me from the tempests of life. Georgia's legacy is a beacon, illuminating my ability to withstand, to endure, and ultimately to thrive."
8. "I am the phoenix, reborn from the ashes of my former self. Each struggle, like those Georgia endured, fuels my ascent, cloaking me in the fiery mantle of resilience."
9. "I walk through fire and emerge unscathed, tempered by the flames of adversity. Georgia's passage through trials lights my way, teaching me that in the heat of challenge, my resilience is forged."
10. "I am a vessel of hope, undeterred by the tempests that seek to drown my spirit. Guided by the beacon of Georgia's resilience, I navigate through storms, my heart an anchor in the shifting sands of life."

Allow these affirmations to be your companions through the journey of existence, a soothing echo of Georgia's resilience that lives within you. In the reflective solitude of personal trials and triumphs, may you find solace in the knowledge that resilience is not just about enduring but about flourishing amidst the rubble of our battles, a testament to the indomitable spirit that resides within each of us.

## Achievement

In the quiet, contemplative hours of dawn, as the world around us whispers of beginnings and the soft light caresses the dreams we dare to live, let us unfold the pages of Georgia's memoir, drawing from her story ten affirmations of achievement. Each word is a testament to the journey, not just of reaching peaks but of embracing the valleys that shape us.

1. "In the symphony of my life, every step forward is a note of triumph, a melody born from the silence of struggle. Like Georgia, I recognize that my achievements are compositions of resilience and dedication, resonating with the harmony of fulfilled dreams."
2. "With every challenge I transcend, I plant the seeds of my legacy, nurturing them with hope and hard work. Georgia's journey teaches me that the gardens of our lives bloom from the soil of our efforts, each flower an emblem of what we have achieved."
3. "I am the sculptor of my success, each decision a chisel marking stone. Inspired by Georgia, I see that my achievements are not just milestones but artworks, defining the landscape of my journey with intention and grace."
4. "Beneath the vast skies of possibility, I stand firmly grounded in my purpose. Georgia's story is a reminder that to reach for the stars, one must build foundations of persistence and passion, each achievement a starlight reflection of our innermost quests."
5. "In the quietude of self-reflection, I find the essence of my achievements. Like Georgia, I understand that true success is

not just an external accolade but an internal affirmation of growth, resilience, and the courage to be authentically me."
6. "Each dawn brings the promise of new achievements. As Georgia navigated the uncertainties of her path, I too embrace the light of each morning, seeing in its arrival the potential to create, achieve, and inspire."
7. "I walk the path of achievement with humility, knowing that every summit reached is also a moment to honor the journey. Georgia's reflections teach me that our greatest accomplishments are often silent, witnessed by the heart and the soul."
8. "My achievements are bridges between my dreams and reality. Drawing courage from Georgia's story, I embark on the construction of these connections with the strength of my convictions, aware that every completed span is a step closer to the essence of my aspirations."
9. "In the tapestry of my achievements, each thread is woven with the colors of perseverance and faith. Georgia's narrative of struggle and success imbues me with the belief that my endeavors, too, can be a masterpiece of dedication and hope."
10. "The echoes of my achievements will resonate beyond the confines of time, a legacy of the spirit's indefatigable quest for fulfillment. Inspired by Georgia, I stride forward, knowing that what I achieve is not just for me but for all who dare to dream and work towards those dreams."

Let these affirmations, born from the reflection of Georgia's life and achievements, be a lighthouse guiding us through the tempests and calms of our own journeys. In the embrace of her story, may we find the courage to carve our paths, to achieve with grace, and to live with the heart's full splendor.

## Confidence

Embark on a transformative journey of self-assurance, inspired by the resilient spirit of Georgia. As we delve into these affirmations, allow them to resonate within, guiding you toward a profound realization of your own unshakeable confidence. These statements are not just phrases; they are stepping stones towards embracing your full potential and thriving in every aspect of life.

1. "I am the architect of my confidence, constructing it brick by brick with the mortar of self-belief." Just as Georgia learned to recognize her worth and reject opportunities that did not align with her goals, so too do I build a fortress of self-assurance, carefully selecting what strengthens my structure.
2. "Each day, I choose to wear my confidence like a finely tailored suit—perfectly fitted to my unique contours of character." Inspired by Georgia's transformation, I remind myself daily of my value and step into each challenge with poise and assurance.
3. "I am fluent in the language of self-confidence; my words and actions resonate with clarity and purpose." Observing Georgia's newfound ability to express herself, I cultivate my own voice with the same conviction and eloquence.
4. "My confidence shines from within, illuminating paths once shadowed by doubt." Georgia's journey of self-realization lights the way for me to tread boldly in areas where I once hesitated.
5. "With each step forward, I plant my feet firmly in the soil of self-assurance, growing taller towards my sunlight." Reflecting on Georgia's progress, I recognize each

advancement in my life as a reinforcement of my own confidence.
6. "I draw strength from the well of my past achievements and sip the sweet water of confidence with each remembrance." As Georgia reflects on her past successes to fuel her self-belief, so do I remind myself of my capabilities and achievements to bolster my confidence.
7. "My confidence is a testament not only to who I am but also to whom I can become." Learning from Georgia's revelations, I see every opportunity for growth as a chance to expand the horizons of my self-assurance.
8. "I navigate the complexities of life with a compass of confidence, guided by the true north of my inner values." Observing the changes in Georgia's life decisions, I, too, let my deepest values steer me through decisions with confidence.
9. "In the reflection of my daily endeavors, I see a portrait of poise and self-respect." Inspired by Georgia's morning routine, I begin each day affirming my worth and capabilities, setting a confident tone for the hours ahead.
10. "My confidence is my shield and my spear—defending against doubt and propelling me forward." Drawing upon Georgia's narrative, I arm myself with an unwavering belief in my skills and potential, ready to confront challenges and seize opportunities.

Let these affirmations serve as your guideposts, illuminating the path to a more confident you. As you traverse this journey, remember that confidence is not merely a gift but a skill—honed through reflection, reinforced by successes, and celebrated in every small victory. Embrace this process, and watch as the world opens before you, ripe with possibility and new horizons to explore.

## Excellence

Drawing upon Georgia's profound journey detailed in her memoir, let us delve into crafting affirmations that weave together strands of excellence and confidence. These affirmations are designed not only to encourage reflection but also to act as catalysts for personal and communal growth. As you engage with each affirmation, remember that excellence is not a distant summit to be scaled, but a path to be walked daily with confidence, purpose, and self-awareness.

1. "I embrace excellence in every action, understanding that each step taken in confidence brings me closer to the highest version of myself." Inspired by Georgia's relentless pursuit of growth, let this affirmation remind you that excellence begins with a commitment to personal development.
2. "With grace and confidence, I overcome challenges, recognizing them as opportunities to demonstrate my resilience and dedication to excellence." As Georgia faced obstacles with courage, use this affirmation to fortify your resolve in the face of adversity.
3. "I hold my vision of excellence with unwavering confidence, allowing it to guide my decisions and actions each day." Georgia's clarity in her goals greatly contributed to her achievements. Let this affirmation be a beacon that keeps your aspirations in clear view.
4. "I cultivate excellence in my interactions, knowing that every connection is a chance to positively influence others and build community." Reflecting on Georgia's impact as a social worker, remember that your actions have the power to uplift and inspire those around you.

5. "My journey towards excellence is fueled by a confidence that is nurtured through continuous learning and self-reflection." Just as Georgia's reflective practice led to profound insights, embrace this affirmation to commit to lifelong learning and growth.
6. "I confidently contribute my best, secure in the knowledge that my efforts are steps towards mastering my craft and exemplifying excellence." Let Georgia's dedication to her profession inspire you to approach your work with the same level of excellence and pride.
7. "I trust in my ability to achieve excellence, allowing this confidence to permeate every challenge I undertake." Georgia's self-belief was key to her successes. Use this affirmation to bolster your trust in your capabilities.
8. "Excellence is my guiding principle, and confidence my companion, as I navigate the complexities of life with poise and purpose." This affirmation is a reminder that your path is defined by the lofty standards you set and the confidence with which you pursue them.
9. "Each day, I celebrate small victories and acknowledge my progress towards excellence, building my confidence and defining my legacy." Georgia's reflections on her achievements highlight the importance of recognizing and valuing each step forward.
10. "I am a beacon of excellence and confidence, inspiring others through my actions and encouraging them to discover their path of greatness." Motivated by Georgia's example, let this affirmation be your commitment to not only pursuing personal excellence but also empowering others to strive for their best.

Embark on your journey with these affirmations as your compass, pointing you towards a life of fulfilled potential and impactful achievements. Each step you take imbued with confidence and guided by excellence will carve pathways for others to follow, enhancing not just your life but also enriching your community.

# Faith

In the spirit of fostering a journey of self-discovery and growth, inspired by the transformative narrative of Georgia, let us immerse ourselves in affirmations that intertwine faith with confidence. These affirmations are crafted to serve as tools for personal empowerment, guiding you to unlock your potential and echo the resilience and faith depicted in Georgia's memoir. Each statement is a stepping stone towards cultivating a fortified sense of self, rooted in faith and radiating confidence.

1. "I anchor my actions in faith and move forward with unwavering confidence, knowing that each step is guided by a higher purpose." Let this affirmation inspire you to trust in your journey and the guidance that shapes it, reinforcing your path with purposeful strides.
2. "Rooted in faith, I embrace my unique gifts with confidence, understanding that they are bestowed upon me to fulfill my mission and serve others." This affirmation encourages you to recognize and utilize your talents as instruments of your personal mission, guided by a deep faith in their purposeful design.
3. "With faith as my shield, I wield confidence as my sword, ready to confront obstacles with grace and emerge stronger." Allow this powerful imagery to remind you that faith and confidence together form an invincible alliance against challenges, leading to growth and resilience.
4. "I nurture my faith, allowing it to bloom alongside my confidence, understanding that together, they illuminate the path to self-discovery and achievement." This affirmation is a gentle prompt to cultivate both faith and confidence,

recognizing their symbiotic relationship in your journey of self-improvement.

5. "My faith fuels my confidence, enabling me to embrace uncertainty with composure and see every challenge as an opportunity for growth." Inspired by Georgia's journey, embrace this affirmation as a testament to the strength derived from faith to face uncertainties with a poised and confident heart.
6. "I trust in the timing of my life, bolstered by faith and propelled by confidence, knowing that I am exactly where I need to be for my highest good." This statement encourages patient trust in your journey, emphasizing that faith and confidence are key to recognizing and embracing life's timing.
7. "I am a beacon of faith and confidence, inspiring those around me to journey towards their fullest potential with courage and trust." Let this affirmation serve as a call to action, to not only journey within but also to illuminate the path for others through your example.
8. "In moments of doubt, I return to my faith, allowing it to restore my confidence and remind me of my inherent strength and purpose." Use this affirmation as a gentle reminder that faith is a reservoir of strength, capable of reigniting your confidence in moments of uncertainty.
9. "I celebrate each victory with gratitude, recognizing them as affirmations of my faith and confidence in action." This affirmation invites you to view your successes as manifestations of your faith and confidence, encouraging a heart of gratitude.
10. "My faith guides me to my truth, and with confidence, I express this truth, fully embracing my authenticity." Embrace this affirmation as an encouragement to live authentically, guided by faith and expressed with confidence, honoring your true self.

As you reflect on these affirmations, let them guide you towards a deeper understanding of your faith and confidence. Remember, the journey you are on is uniquely yours. Both faith and confidence are your companions, aiding in the uncovering of your true potential and the realization of your aspirations. Embrace them, and let them propel you forward, towards a life of fulfillment and purpose.

## Persistence

Embracing the essence of Georgia's memoir, let us craft affirmations that encapsulate the virtues of persistence and confidence. Reflect on these affirmations—each one a stepping stone for your personal odyssey towards self-reliance and communal contribution. Through persistence and confidence, you become the architect of your destiny, constructing a legacy of resilience, determination, and unwavering self-assurance.

1. "I am persistent in my pursuits, bolstered by a confidence that grows with every challenge I overcome." May this affirmation remind you that each hurdle surmounted adds a robust layer to your confidence.
2. "With each set back, my resolve is strengthened, and my confidence deepened, knowing that persistence carves the path to success." Utilize this affirmation as a mantra, transforming temporary defeats into enduring triumphs of learning and fortitude.
3. "Confidence is my constant companion on this journey of persistence; together we turn aspirations into achievements." Let this affirmation affirm the duo of persistence and confidence as fundamental companions on your voyage towards self-actualization.
4. "My commitment to my goals is unwavering; my confidence unshakable. In steadfast persistence, I find my power." With this affirmation, stand tall in the knowledge that your tenacity is an inexhaustible source of strength.
5. "Every persistent step I take builds the staircase to my success, upon which my confidence ascends." Allow this affirmation to

visualize each effort contributing constructively to the grand design of your life's ambitions.
6. "I trust in my ability to persist, for within me is a reservoir of confidence that knows no bounds." This affirmation serves as a reminder that the wellspring of confidence within you is both boundless and replenishable through perseverance.
7. "I embrace the process, persistent in action and poised in confidence, for I am the master of my own progress." Embrace this affirmation as a declaration of self-governance and continuous advancement.
8. "Persistence is my pledge, confidence my declaration, and together they forge the armor against all odds." May this affirmation equip you with an indomitable spirit as you journey through the tapestry of experiences life presents.
9. "The echoes of my persistence resound with confidence, as I celebrate each small victory on the road to greatness." Let this affirmation be a joyful incantation, highlighting the importance of recognizing every step that edges you closer to your goals.
10. "In the heart of uncertainty, my confidence rallies, fueling my persistence to press onward towards my envisioned future." With this affirmation, affirm that even in ambiguity, your conviction and determination remain unyielded, steering you towards your desired horizon.

Remember, affirmations are deeply personal instruments of inner dialogue. Let these words not merely be recited, but internalized, breathed into life through your actions and reflections. As you walk this path, may your persistence be as resilient as the mountains and your confidence as vast as the skies. You are the sculptor of your reality; mold it with purpose, intention, and unfaltering self-belief.

## Leverage

In the spirit of Georgia's remarkable journey of self-discovery and mastery, captured in the depths of her memoir, we present to you affirmations crafted to ignite and leverage your inner confidence. This journey is not merely about reaching a destination but about unfolding the grandeur within you, piece by piece. Utilize these affirmations as tools to sculpt your path, to build bridges towards your aspirations, and to empower your steps with confidence. Each affirmation is designed to be both a mirror, reflecting your innermost potential, and a beacon, guiding your way through the mists of doubt and uncertainty.

1. "I hold the power to shape my destiny; my confidence is the chisel I use to sculpt my future." Let this affirmation remind you that your confidence is a transformative force, capable of molding the very fabric of your reality.
2. "With every breath, I inhale confidence and exhale hesitation; each step I take is grounded in a deep sense of self-assurance." Utilize this affirmation as a rhythmic mantra, syncing your actions with the pulse of unfaltering confidence.
3. "I illuminate the rooms I enter with my confidence, inspiring others to find their own light within." Adopt this affirmation as a testament to the influential power of your presence, a beacon that not only guides your path but also lights the way for others.
4. "Each challenge I face is an opportunity to reaffirm my confidence and fortify my resolve." Let this statement serve as a reminder that obstacles are not barriers, but catalysts for growth, each one strengthening the foundation of your confidence.

5. "I am a master of my thoughts; I choose confidence as my lens through which the world becomes a realm of possibilities." Embrace this affirmation to cultivate a mindset where confidence reigns, transforming your perspectives and unlocking doors to endless opportunities.
6. "My confidence is unwavering, not because I never fall, but because I always choose to rise." Use this affirmation to acknowledge that true confidence stems not from infallibility, but from resilience and the undying will to persevere.
7. "In the symphony of life, my confidence is the melody that dances boldly in the face of adversity." Let this affirmation inspire you to move through life with a rhythm that resonates with courage, grace, and self-assurance.
8. "I command my space with confidence, not out of arrogance, but from a deep-rooted belief in my own value and capabilities." This affirmation is a declaration of self-esteem, urging you to occupy your space proudly, grounded in the knowledge of your worth.
9. "My confidence is my shield; it guards my dreams and fuels my journey towards actualizing them." Adopt this affirmation as both a protective mantra and a driving force, empowering you to chase your dreams with vigor and determination.
10. "I pledge to nurture my confidence daily, understanding that it is the soil in which my greatest potential can flourish." Utilize this affirmation as a commitment to self-growth, recognizing that a well-tended garden of confidence is where your true potential blooms.

As you reflect on these affirmations, inspired by the resilience and self-realization journey of Georgia, remember that your confidence is not a static trait but a dynamic force. It grows, it transforms, and it adapts, much like you. Leverage it as the powerful tool it is, allowing it to propel you towards your aspirations with conviction and grace.

You are the sculptor of your destiny; wield your confidence with purpose and intention, and watch as the world shapes itself around the masterpiece that is you.

# Learning

In the spirit of Georgia's journey through healing and self-realization, we recognize that learning confidence is both a process and a practice. Embarking on this path requires patience, reflection, and a steadfast commitment to nurturing one's innate abilities and strengths. The following affirmations are designed to serve as guideposts, illuminating the path to learning confidence with intention and wisdom. They are stepping stones to discovering the profound impact of self-belief and the transformative power of confidence in one's learning journey. Each affirmation is an invitation to pause, reflect, and embrace the potential that resides within you, waiting to be unlocked and shared with the world.

1. "I embrace each learning opportunity with an open heart and mind, knowing that with each step, my confidence is being built." Let this affirmation encourage you to approach learning with curiosity and openness, recognizing each experience as a foundation upon which confidence is constructed.
2. "I trust in my ability to grow and learn from every situation, confident that I am gaining invaluable insights along the way." Use this affirmation to reinforce your intrinsic ability to learn and adapt, acknowledging that confidence is cultivated through embracing the process of learning.
3. "My potential to succeed is limitless when I support it with a confident belief in my capability to learn and evolve." This affirmation is a reminder of your boundless potential when underpinned by a solid foundation of confidence in your own abilities.
4. "I view challenges as rich soil for growth, affirming my confidence to learn and flourish in adversity." Let this

affirmation transform your perspective on challenges, seeing them as opportunities to strengthen your confidence and resilience.
5. "Every day, I commit to learning something new, bolstering my confidence through the power of knowledge and experience." Use this affirmation as a daily commitment to personal growth and learning, understanding that confidence is nurtured through continuous effort and discovery.
6. "I give myself permission to make mistakes, learning from them with confidence and grace." This affirmation encourages a healthy relationship with failure, recognizing that mistakes are invaluable learning opportunities that contribute to your confidence.
7. "With confidence, I celebrate my progress, no matter how small, knowing that each step forward enriches my journey of learning." Let this affirmation be a reminder to honor and celebrate every achievement, understanding that each contributes to building a more confident self.
8. "I confidently share my insights and learnings, knowing that my unique perspective adds value to the collective wisdom." Use this affirmation to boost your confidence in contributing your knowledge and experiences, appreciating the impact of your unique voice in collective learning.
9. "I am patient and gentle with myself on my learning journey, trusting that confidence grows at its own pace." This affirmation serves as a gentle nudge to practice self-compassion and patience, recognizing that the development of confidence is a personal and non-linear journey.
10. "Each question I ask, each answer I seek, strengthens my confidence in my journey of discovery and understanding." Let this affirmation encourage an inquisitive mindset, affirming that the pursuit of knowledge itself is an act of confidence.

By embracing these affirmations, you are not only committing to a journey of learning confidence but also to a deeper process of self-discovery and personal growth. Remember, confidence is not a destination but a way of being, cultivated through each step of your learning journey. As you reflect upon and integrate these affirmations into your daily practice, may you find your path illuminated with the confidence that comes from knowing and believing in yourself and your abilities.

## Courage

Drawing inspiration from Georgia's memoir, a narrative rich with challenges and triumphs, these affirmations are crafted to embolden you on your journey toward greater courage. Courage often manifests in the face of the unknown and the uncomfortable, encouraging growth and fostering resilience. Embedded within Georgia's experiences are powerful lessons on facing fear, embracing vulnerability, and taking bold steps forward. These affirmations, rooted in systematic development and introspection, are designed to be stepping stones that guide and fortify your path to living courageously.

1. "I embrace the strength within me to step into the unknown, trusting that each step forward fortifies my courage." Use this affirmation to affirm your inner strength and your capability to navigate through uncharted territories.
2. "I confront my fears with an open heart and mind, understanding that true growth comes from vulnerability and courage." This affirmation is a call to embrace your fears as gateways to transformation and self-discovery.
3. "With each act of courage, I dismantle the barriers of fear that have held me back, freeing myself to live authentically." Let this be a reminder that your acts of bravery are powerful catalysts for change, inspiring you to live your truth.
4. "I allow myself to be vulnerable, knowing that in vulnerability lies the courage to truly connect and grow." This affirmation encourages you to see vulnerability not as weakness, but as a profound strength that fosters genuine connections and personal growth.

5. "I choose to respond to challenges with courage, using them as stepping stones to build a resilient and fearless version of myself." Use this to transform challenges into opportunities, each one an invitation to become more courageous and resilient.
6. "I lead my life with courage, inspiring others around me to step out of their comfort zones and pursue their dreams." Adopt this affirmation to not only cultivate your own courage but also to become a beacon of inspiration for others.
7. "Every day, I commit to small acts of courage, knowing that they accumulate to create significant change." This affirmation emphasizes that courage doesn't always roar; sometimes, it's the quiet voice at the end of the day reminding you to keep going.
8. "I trust in the power of my own courage, allowing it to propel me forward in my journey of self-realization and community building." Let this serve as a testament to the strength of your courage and its ability to propel you toward deeper insights and broader impacts.
9. "I celebrate each courageous decision I make, recognizing them as milestones in my journey of self-empowerment." Use this affirmation to honor and celebrate your choices that require courage, seeing them as pivotal moments of empowerment.
10. "I nurture my spirit with encouraging thoughts and actions that bolster my courage and elevate my journey." This affirmation is an invitation to continuously support yourself with thoughts and actions that enhance your courage, uplifting your entire journey.

By integrating these affirmations into your daily practice, you are taking a systematic and introspective approach to cultivating courage. Each affirmation is designed not just to inspire but also to encourage you to take active steps in recognizing and overcoming the barriers that fear may present. Let each affirmation be a bridge to greater understanding of your inner strength, and a guide toward a more courageous, empowered life.

# Adaptability

These 10 affirmations for adaptability are crafted to support your journey through change and uncertainty. Georgia's memoir serves as a valuable inspiration, illustrating the power of adaptability in navigating life's manifold paths. Each affirmation prompts not only reflection but also enkindles a proactive embrace of adaptability as a cornerstone of growth and success.

1. "I greet change with a poised heart, ready to weave resilience into the fabric of my being." Let this affirmation be your compass as you navigate the ebb and flow of circumstances, fostering resilience through an adaptability that's both reflexive and intentional.
2. "Adaptability is my natural state; I am fluid, flexible, and open to the wealth of possibilities that change brings." This affirmation encourages you to view adaptability not as a challenge, but as an innate quality that unlocks potential and opportunities.
3. "With each shift in my journey, my adaptability becomes a bridge, connecting present challenges to future triumphs." Use this to remind yourself that adaptability is a transformative force, turning any hurdle into a stepping stone for success.
4. "I have the power to thrive in transience, embracing change as a catalyst for innovation and growth." Allow this affirmation to inspire confidence in your ability to not just survive, but thrive amidst change.

5. "I am equipped with the wisdom to recognize that adaptability is not about losing myself; it is about evolving with purpose." This affirmation calls on you to evolve with intention, knowing that adaptability is an ally in your personal and communal endeavors.
6. "Through the lens of adaptability, every unexpected turn is reframed as a path to new skills and deeper insights." Embrace this viewpoint to transform the unforeseen into opportunities for learning and self-discovery.
7. "I choose to view adaptability as a form of self-empowerment, taking charge of change and molding it to my aspirations." Use this affirmation as a testament to adaptability being a proactive choice, a form of empowerment that aligns with your goals.
8. "Adaptability allows me to engage constructively with change, seeing it as a dance where I am both a participant and a choreographer." Let this inspire you to take an active role in the ever-changing dance of life, contributing to the rhythm of change.
9. "In the face of transition, my adaptability is the compass that guides me to my North Star of principles and values." This affirmation reinforces that adaptability is both guided by and reinforces your core principles and values.
10. "I am a testament to the strength of adaptability, transforming every challenge into a demonstration of my capacity to prevail." Embrace this as a declaration of your resilience, showing that adaptability is the embodiment of your enduring spirit.

With these affirmations, you are invited to recognize adaptability as a dynamic and empowering asset, essential for personal development and community building. Embrace adaptability as both a skill and a philosophy, one that enriches your existence and enhances your contributions to the collective whole. Reflect upon these affirmations, integrate them into your practice, and witness the profound impact adaptability has on your journey to realizing your utmost potential.

## Networking

In the silent spaces between us, where connections are woven invisibly and profoundly, Georgia's journey from her memoir whispers to us about the essence of networking—it's not about collecting people, but about planting the seeds of relationships that might one day bloom into something extraordinary. Each of these affirmations is a petal in the garden of our interactions, a gentle reminder of the delicate yet robust nature of human connection.

1. "I step into new circles with my authenticity as my emblem, my vulnerability my strength, ever willing to grow my world by one meaningful exchange at a time." Let this affirmation be a guide, encouraging you to embrace your true self as you forge new connections.
2. "Like a tree extending its branches, I reach out with genuine intent, knowing that every leaf I touch may someday turn to gold in the currency of kinship." This affirmation invites you to network with purpose, not just for the advancement it may bring, but for the richness it adds to the tapestry of your experiences.
3. "In the ebb and flow of dialogue, I am both a listener and a storyteller, cultivating a garden where sympathy and stories can blossom in kindred spirits." Use this to remind yourself that networking is an exchange, where giving attention is as important as commanding it.
4. "I honor the bridges burnt and paths diverged, for they too have shaped the labyrinth of my journey, leading me to people and places where my spirit finds solace and strength." Embrace this affirmation as a reflection on loss and growth in your networking journey.

5. "I weave through the cacophony of voices with discernment, aligning my orbit with those stars whose light complements my own, progressing from solitude to solidarity." This affirmation encourages the selective forming of connections that enhance and echo your inner values.
6. "Networking, a delicate dance of progress and pause, where every 'no' I pronounce carves space for a 'yes' that resonates with the vibration of my purpose." Allow this affirmation to be about mindful growth, understanding that every refusal paves the way for a more aligned commitment.
7. "As I traverse the terrain of my field, each handshake is a seed planted in the soil of possibility, tended with patience and the promise of tomorrow's harvest." Reflect on this as an encouragement to network with a long-term perspective of nurturing each relationship.
8. "I honor the memory of connections lost, a sea of faces past, for even in their fleeting presence, they imparted lessons deep as the ocean's uncharted depths." This affirmation acknowledges the transient nature of some relationships and the enduring impact they leave behind.
9. "With the silent hymn of empathy, I approach new connections, understanding that beneath every professional façade, a personal story awaits to be heard." Use this to reinforce the value of empathy in networking, creating more profound and personal bonds.
10. "I honor the mosaic of my network, each connection a piece of stained glass, disparate yet together creating a vibrant tableau of my journey thus far." Let this affirmation celebrate the diverse and colorful spectrum of your relationships, each adding unique beauty to the collective picture.

In the spirit of Georgia's memoir, let these affirmations for networking remind you that behind every exchange there is a potential for a story to unfold, a lesson to learn, and a relationship to treasure. Networking, then, becomes less about strategy and more about humanity—an art form that, when done with sincerity and heart, can transform the professional into the personal, and acquaintances into allies.

www.ingramcontent.com/pod-product-compliance
Lightning Source LLC
Chambersburg PA
CBHW070203100426
42743CB00013B/3032